3-5-3
DEFENSE
FOR
YOUTH
AND
MIDDLE SCHOOL
FOOTBALL

A PRACTICAL COACHING GUIDE

This book was developed by Coach James "Pop" Saylor, with Coach James "Jim" Saylor, Jr.

ISBN: 978-0-578-01680-1

Visit: www.thebusinesscoach.org

The Business Coach

TheBusinessCoach.org

CONTENTS

ACKNOWLEDGEMENTS

Over the years, we collected many ideas, processes, procedures, instructions and drills. We learned over the years from many dedicated coaches that shared their information. It is impossible to acknowledge all of these dedicated people that provide valuable football information to grow the sport.

Thanks to Mike Falcone and Greg Bowman for their vision in installing the 3-5-3 defense at the high school.

Special thanks to Scott Douglas. Scotty was a player for the middle school team the first year we introduced the 3-5-3 defense. He was a coach on the field for a couple of years.

NOTE: A good basic reference for the 3-5-3 defense at any level is the Video Series by Championship Productions by Taylor Burks of Georgia Military.

FORWARD

This book is the result of many years of involvement in youth football as a player, parent, coach and administrator. Between by son and me, we have over 60 years of experience that spans several generations. I played in the sixties. My son played and I coached in the seventies. I coached in the eighties for my other son while junior played high school and college football. We have both coached my two grandsons since 2001. In addition, we both have been administrators over the years in various youth leagues. This is a truly unique experience. This is the tradition we would like to continue for generations of families into the future.

Over the years, we used the traditional youth football defenses. Five years ago we started using the 3-5-3 defense for the middle school team. This was the result of the high school adopting this defense. We were mandated to use the 3-5-3 for the middle school. The results have been exceptional. The defensive statistics are unbelievable. We made progress on the field every year and we even had an undefeated season.

For the youth league, each team could use any defense. This was usually the 5-4, 6-2, 4-4 or 4-3 defenses. We tried to install the 3-5-3 defense with several youth teams. Because it was new to other youth coaches, we usually installed it with other defenses or we compromised some of the 3-5-3 defense.. With the youth teams, we did not have as much success using the 3-5-3 until the year when we won the league championship. We learned a lot both from the failures and the success.

This book is about what we learned to successfully implement the 3-5-3 defense at the youth and middle school level. We believe the 3-5-3 defense is the perfect defense for these levels of football. First of all it produces results. Second, it is appropriate for all type of players. Third, it works against the run and pass, but it is particularly good against the run. Fourth, it causes confusion on the offense which gives the defense some edge. Fifth, most importantly, the 3-5-3 is fun for the players. Sixth, it is easy to teach the players. Finally, it strengthens the team. In many youth football teams, the defense is looked at as not being as prestigious as the offense. The 3-5-3 defense allows the defense to shine along with the offense.

INTRODUCTION

The book serves as a manual for any youth and middle school coach wishing to achieve victory. Victory in this book does not mean championships or even wins. We focus on the pursuit of victory. This is our philosophy for success. As a result of focusing on our view of VICTORY, we have achieved success on the field in terms of championships and wins. VICTORY means the following:

- ➢ Players have positive football experiences
- ➢ Players learn the fundamentals of football
- ➢ Players have fun
- ➢ Players want to play football
- ➢ Players are better people
- ➢ Players give maximum effort
- ➢ Players improve their football skills
- ➢ Players learn sportsmanship
- ➢ Players value teamwork
- ➢ Players learn about themselves
- ➢ Players enjoy the game and return to play
- ➢ Players are VICTORS

VICTORS

VICTORS focus on success and have the desire, determination and discipline to succeed.

VICTORS are confident and they always give their best.

VICTORS are team players that care for, support and encourage teammates.

VICTORS never let their teammates down. They value winning as a team and they do whatever is necessary for the good of the team.

VICTORS are excellent in their performance on the field.

VICTORS never give up in competition.

VICTORS always strive for victory and they view losing as an opportunity for improvement.

VICTORS take pride in their accomplishments as a team.

VICTORS have respect for coaches, teammates and opponents.

VICTORS are passionate about football.

VICTORS approach any challenge with maximum effort, excitement and enthusiasm.

VICTORS are aggressive, high energy and always hustle.

VICTORS play football to have fun and win or lose display good sportsmanship with their head held high.

VICTORS will overcome obstacles.

VICTORS play with passion and pride.

We are **VICTORS** and we expect VICTORY.

You may ask "What does the above have to do with the 3-5-3 defense?" Success with the 3-5-3 defense, as with almost any other worthwhile endeavor in life, starts with a FOCUS. The focus is the ultimate view of victory. The focus is the cause that rallies minds and hearts. The focus provides promise, purpose and passion. Without a focus, you will never be successful. A focus includes many elements. It encompasses your dreams, views, values, and goals. These are usually formally or informally expressed as vision, mission, philosophy, principles, and values. Written or unwritten, your focus impacts every aspect of your program. The focus is part of the foundation section of this book. The foundation builds the system for the 3-5-3 defense. It is not all about X's and O's. We can directly attribute our failures in implementing the 3-5-3 at the youth level to elements in the foundation. We had a foundation with the high school for the middle school program. At the youth level, coaches, administrators and some parents did not believe in our focus. This was the difference between failure and success. You must develop the foundation as described in chapter 1.

The other sections in this book focus on the Xs and Os and the players. You must be a player-focused coach. This defense allows young players to develop and use fundamental football skills. Players love the aggressive style of the defense. They also appreciate the discipline. This combination of aggressive style, with need for discipline, works best in a positive, encouraging environment.

The essence of the 3-5-3 defense is attack. With this focus, the outline of this book is ATTACK which is as follows:

Align Players

Teach Responsibilities

Train Fundamentals

Allow Fun

Coach Game Day

Keep It Simple

CHAPTER 1
DEVELOPING THE FOUNDATION

Victory! We all want it. We are continuously looking for ways to achieve victory. In the introduction, we describe our view of VICTORY. Over the years, the VICTORY system has been used to create high performing organizations. We use the VICTORY system as our model for our football program. The VICTORY system as shown in figure 1 is as follows:

Visioning creates a common focus

Involving everyone establishes a superior organization/team

Continuously improving achieves excellence

Training, educating, and coaching develops a learning culture

Owning the performance fosters empowerment

Recognizing and rewarding builds high performance

Yearning ensures success

     Players drive VICTORY

     Coaches through leadership guide VICTORY

LEADERSHIP

Visioning

Yearning for VICTORY

Involving Everyone

Recognizing and Rewarding

TEAM/PLAYERS

Continuously Improving

Owing Performance

Training, Educating Coaching

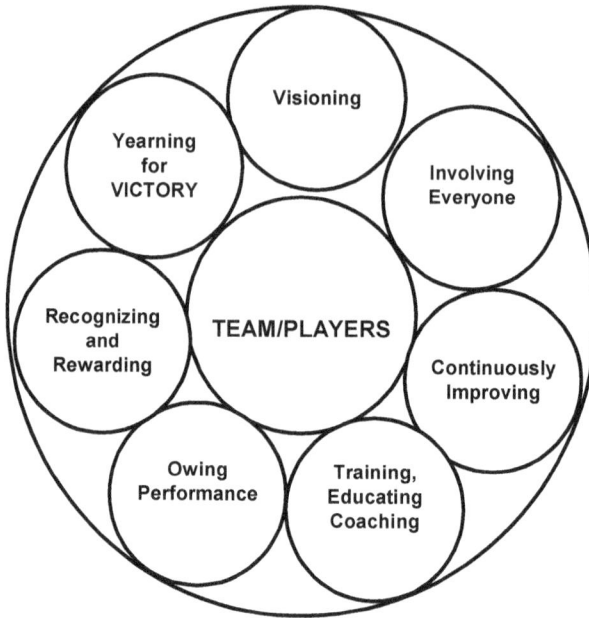

Figure 1. VICTORY Model.

For the purpose of this book, we will only highlight critical points for VICTORY in youth and middle school football. The vision is critical to any successful football program. It impacts every aspect of the program. The head coach, the assistant coaches and players must have a common focus for the team.

Involving everyone, every player, every coach, and parents will make the team work. The team must maximize each persons' (coaches and players) individual talents. Also, the team must function together. Teamwork must be worked continuously and individual talent must be developed constantly. All stakeholders must be included in the team.

Continuous improvement is the essence of youth and middle school football. Day after day each player must get better. In addition, this means coaches must also improve everyday. They must provide the drills and techniques to ensure a constant forward movement for each individual player and the team as a whole.

Football is learning. The players and coaches are forever gaining knowledge, learning new skills. There is always something new, interesting and exciting to learn. The coaches need to understand the importance of using various methods for learning to include training, educating, and coaching, In addition, they must know when the techniques are appropriate in the football setting. Educating is used for knowledge. Training is best for skills and coaching is most appropriate for the game.

Ownership of performance is important. Coaches must feel they own their specific role and responsibilities for the team. Specifically, this means the head coach must not micromanage the assistant coaches. They must have the power to coach. In addition, the players must also be empowered to perform at his/her best.

High performance is motivated by appropriate recognition. Each coach must look for the positive and give praise when it is deserved by the player. Rewards at the youth level need to be considered in light of individual self-esteem and the effect on teamwork. You must use a method that is fair and consistent. We have found helmet decals, most valuable players awards and player of the game awards can be counterproductive at the youth level and middle school level However, team oriented rewards can be productive.

First, all coaches must have a passion for the game. This passion needs to be instilled in the players. In order for football to be the sport of choice of our youth, it has to be about the future of the game.

Players drive victory. The focus must be on the players. It is not about the coaches or the parents. It must always be about the players.

Leadership must first come from the coaches. At the youth level it is difficult to have player leaders. However, at the middle school level some players can be expected to be leaders.

VICTORY

In summary, the above can be shown as in figure 2 being a combination of organizational excellence plus player focus plus leadership equals VICTORY.

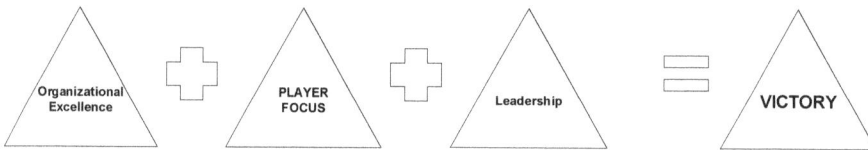

Figure 2. VICTORY Summary

COACHING POINT: VICTORY is achieved by focusing on each of the elements. Victory is the result.

Organizational Excellence

Organizational excellence starts with the basic foundation. Figure 3 below shows the elements of the foundation. Integrity, trust and credibility form the baseline. Care is essential. Communication is critical, and belief is decisive for success.

Figure 3. Organizational Foundation

Foundation

The foundation provides the environment for VICTORY. The VICTORY foundation follows:

Fosters openness, fairness, and sincerity

Operates with honesty

Uses common sense

Nurtures trust

Demonstrates appropriate behavior

Allows involvement by everyone

Teaches right from wrong

Instills values

Only do to others what you would want done to you

Never compromise ethics, integrity, or trust

Integrity

A person's true nature will reveal itself despite disguise.

Integrity implies honesty, morals, values, fairness, adherence to the facts, and sincerity. This characteristic is what anyone expects and deserves to receive. It also means consistency.

Identify your value system

Normalize values within team

Tell the truth

Establish right and wrong behavior

Give respect

Reward appropriate behavior

Instill loyalty

Treat everyone with fairness

Yearn for consistency

Trust

Trust is everything.

Trust is a byproduct of a coach's conduct. Trust is absolutely essential for success. Trust starts with open and honest communication. This is necessary for involvement of the right people in the process. Trust fosters full participation of all members.

Treat others as you want to be treated

Respect others

Understand others' points of view

Set a positive example

Take the initiative/action to communicate honestly

Credibility

Always be at least one step ahead of the players.

Credibility means you are believable. If you are not believable, you cannot achieve VICTORY or success with your organization, team or players. The following are some characteristics that promote credibility.

Confidence

Reasonable

Expertise

Diligence

Intelligence

Beliefs

Likeable

Experience

Care

Players will perform for a coach that cares.

The foundation of integrity, trust and credibility provide the baseline that supports the care element. You must care about the team, especially the players. The following actions can show that you care:

Communicate, especially listen

Attend to each player

Respect each player

Encourage long-term constructive relationships

Communication

Actions speak louder than words—Talk the talk and walk the talk.

Communication is the most important tool in any organization/team. The scope and level of communication increases because VICTORY demands a free flow of information. The success of any organization demands communicating with and among all organization members, players, parents and the community. It requires frequent and effective communications. It demands communication both inside and outside the organization. The coach needs information to understand the needs and expectations of the organization. They need information from each other to achieve organizational excellence. They rely on information from players. There must be constant communication between administrators, coaches, players, parents and community members. Communication coupled with the sharing of the right information is vital. The following are communication tips:

Clarify the message

Observe body language

Maintain everyone's self-esteem

Make your point short and simple

Understand others' points of view

Nurture others' feelings

Involve yourself in the message

Comprehend the message

Attend to the message of others

Talk judiciously

Emphasize listening

As part of communication, feedback is critical. The following outlines some guidelines on effective feedback:

Foster an environment conducive to sharing feedback

Encourage feedback as a matter of routine

Establish guidelines for providing feedback

Discuss all unclear communications, paraphrase and summarize

Be direct with feedback

Ask questions to get a better understanding

Consider "real" feelings of team members

Keep focused on the mission

Listening is the most important part of communication. The following are steps in active listening:

Let others convey their message

Involve yourself in the message

Summarize and paraphrase frequently

Talk only to clarify

Empathize with others' views

Nurture active listening skills

Believe

Finally, players must BELIEVE in the system, coaches and other players. This provides the focus for success. The following provides the focus to believe:

Believe we are winners

Encourage team

Learn to be our best everyday

Inspire by leadership

Empower coaches and players

Visualize success

Enjoy the football experience

Plan for Organizational Excellence

Every organization must have a plan for organizational excellence to include vision, mission, philosophy, principles, objectives and goals.

Victory Vision

VICTORY starts with believing in yourself, your teammates, and your coaches.

VICTORY is practicing perfect.

VICTORY is always being at the right place at the right time. It is making the right play at all times. It is helping your team by helping teammates as well as helping yourself.

VICTORY is bearing down all the way and bearing down twice as hard when the game or practice gets tough.

VICTORY is playing with your head as well as your body. It is in the doing. It is in the action. It is making football PLAYS.

VICTORY is always knowing in a game (or game situation practice) the following:

- ✌ SCORE
- ✌ DOWN
- ✌ DISTANCE
- ✌ YOUR RESPONSIBILITIES

REMEMBER

No team ever walked to VICTORY

ABOVE ALL

Football is a team game. Help one another at all times

Mission

Our mission is a VICTORY football program. The football program is the focus of VICTORY. Without a football program, there is no VICTORY. Your football program considerations include:

Prepare the program

Recognize the importance of people to the program

Organize the program

Guide the program

Require a football system

Allow for changes to the program

Maintain the program

Philosophy of Excellence

Our goal is for everyone on the team to have a fun and rewarding football experience. Of primary importance is the enjoyment of the sport of football. Of equal value is the improvement of every participant, as a player and as a person. The coaches will focus their efforts on improving each individual football player's skills and creating the best team possible.

Winning is not as important as doing our best. We will always play to do our best. We will accept winning and defeat with the same dignity, enjoy the game, learn from success and mistakes and go out and play with enthusiasm in our next game.

Our philosophy includes:

Pursue fun

Have a player-driven focus

Instill team spirit

Lead by positive example

Orient everyone toward excellence

Stress optimum performance

Observe individual differences

Promote sportsmanship

Have parents' involvement

Yearn for a rewarding football experience

We believe in the following principles:

Pursue constant improvement

Require a focus on football

Implement positive discipline

Never use physical activities for punishment

Coach football fundamentals

Include life skills

Plan, prepare and practice

Limit standing around

Encourage teamwork with everyone playing

Success for every member of the team

Teamwork

Together Everyone Achieves More.

Teamwork is the technique where individual team members work together to achieve a COMMON goal or mission. This involves cooperative relationships, open communications, group problem solving, and team decision-making. Teamwork can only be effective in an environment of honesty, trust, open communications, individual involvement, pride of workmanship, and commitment.

Teamwork Considerations

Trust

Effective communication, especially listening

Attitude positive "can do"

Motivation to perform and improve

We mentality

Ownership

Respect and consideration of others

Keeping focus

PLAYER FOCUS

Today's world is radically different from the recent past. It's a new environment where old solutions no longer work. The "same old way" simply does not bring about the necessary results. The coaching paradigm (mind-set) must change to reflect the reality of today's world in order to achieve success.

The "old school" coaching style of tearing down a player and then building him/her back up does not work. Yelling at a player today frequently just shuts down the player to the learning lesson. The "new school" coach must use different techniques to achieve many of the requirements of discipline and teamwork that are essential to a winning football team.

Some of the major considerations in today's world compared with yesterday's issues are discussed below. These conditions require -- no, demand -- change.

- Players are more selective with an increasing amount of options for their time
- Players require a positive experience
- Players expect structure
- Players have more parental pressures

The following are guidelines for becoming player focused:

Pursue a positive environment

Let all players participate

Acknowledge individual differences

Yearn for open and honest communication

Enhance self-esteem

Reinforce progress

Players Attitude

Attitude is everything

Players' attitude plays a part in the success of a player focused coach. The difference between success and failure in football is usually in the mind and heart of the players. Players with a proper attitude are the key to success of the individual player and the team.

Attitude is the difference between winners and losers. A positive, "can do," enthusiastic, helping, caring, empathic, "do anything," mindset makes a winning organization. The following shows a proper attitude.

Act positively

Try for excellence always

Take time to care

Instill confidence in your abilities

Take time to build teamwork

Use every opportunity

Do something special

Enjoy helping teammates

Team Rules

Respect team members, coaches, teachers and parents

Understand your responsible to teammates, be on time, learn football, be prepared

Listen to coaches; NEVER talk while a coach is talking

Encourage teammates; NEVER criticize another player

Strive to do your best at practice, in games and at school

Leadership

As in every organization, the football team requires effective leadership. As a minimum the head coach must be a leader. Ideally, other coaches and even players should display leadership qualities. The following are essential qualities of a leader:

Lead by example

Establish a common purpose

Act to develop a superior organization

Drive excellence

Enhance others

Reinforce progress

CHAPTER 2
BASICS FOR 3-5-3 DEFENSE

Defense wins championships. This is true at any level from pro sports, college, high school, middle school and the youth level. If a team does not score, the team cannot win the game.

With many different defenses to choose at the youth and middle school level, why use the 3-5-3. The following are reasons to use the 3-5-3 defense:

Results (wins, defensive goals)

Enables All Types of Players

Stops Run and Pass

Unglues Offenses

Let's Players Have Fun

Teaching It Is Easy

Strengthens "TEAM"

Besides the above reasons the 3-5-3 defense is a winning defense. There are many successful teams that use the 3-5-3 defense. We have experienced at the youth and middle school, that this defense is a winning defense. Our statistics prove the improvement in every goal and at every level. We will not give statistics in this book. There is evidence at every level that the 3-5-3 defense is a winning defense. The 3-5-3 defense requires discipline. Everyone in the defense must provide maximum effort for success. The fundamentals are the keys. It requires execution. It nurtures every athlete. It is simple to learn and most of all it is enjoyable. The 3-5-3 has the following characteristics of a winning defense:

Discipline

Effort

Fundamentals

Execution

Nurture

Simple

Enjoyable

BASIC DEFENSE

DEFENSE = VICTORY

No team can win if they do not score

PRIMARY DEFENSE OBJECT IVE

Prevent touchdowns

Defense wins ball games. The opponent cannot win if they cannot score.

In most cases, teams do not win games the other team loses the game because of mistakes. The primary objective of the DEFENSE is to stop touchdowns.

Always

➤ Play with excitement, enthusiasm, effort = DESIRE.
➤ Go full speed on every play.
➤ Every defensive player must pursue the ball on every play.
➤ Always pursue on a collision course. Never pursue directly behind a person on your own team.
➤ Gang tackle. First person get in front of runner to stop him. Others go for the BALL and tackle.
➤ Protect you gap first, and then PURSUE the ball carrier.
➤ Get rid of blocker as soon as possible, and then PURSUE the ball carrier.
➤ Use your HANDS.
➤ Get tackle on BLITZ.
➤ Try to knock the ball loose.
➤ Be tough, aggressive and ATTACKING.
➤ COMMUNICATE.

Never

❖ Play with the blocker.
❖ Be a sucker for reverse.
❖ Bury your head down.
❖ Grab facemask or helmet.
❖ Tackle with head down or alligator tackle.
❖ Trip another player to bring them down.
❖ Horse collar a runner.
❖ Stop until you hear the whistle.
❖ Spear another player by using the top of your helmet.
❖ Relax, you can be hit even after the whistle.

Defense Goals

– Create turnovers – interception, fumbles
– Minus yards on plays by offense
– No BIG plays - play over 20 yards
– Sacks
– SCORE! SCORE! SCORE!
– Have **FUN**

KEYS TO THE 3-5-3 DEFENSE

The 3-5-3 defense is an excellent defense against the run and the pass. It is an attacking and aggressive defense. The keys to the 3-5-3 defense include:

Attack on Every Play

Get Physical and Quick

Relentless Pursuit

Emphasize the Blitz

Stop the Run First

Stop BIG Plays

Increase Turnovers

Value Communication

Expect Excellence

3-5-3 Attack Defense

The following chapters will describe the major elements for implementing the 3-5-3 defense at the youth and middle school level.

Align players

Teach gap responsibilities

Train fundamentals

Allow fun

Coach game day

Keep it simple

CHAPTER 3
ALIGN PLAYERS

ALIGN PLAYERS

This defense requires an understanding of the basic positions and the alignment of players. This chapter outlines the following:

Acknowledge the basic 3-5-3 Defense

Learn the positions

Identify the 3-5-3 alignment

Gear alignment to your team

Nominate players for positions

ACKNOWLEDGE THE BASIC 3-5-3 DEFENSE

The basic 3-5-3 defense is shown in figure 4 below. The 3-5-3 defense consists of the following positions.

- 3 Defensive Lineman
  - Nose Guard
  - Defensive Ends (2) (left and right defensive end)
- 5 Linebackers
  - Inside Stack Linebackers (3)
  - Outside Linebackers (2)
- 3 Defensive Backs
  - Corner Backs (2)(left and right corner backs)
  - Free Safety (1)

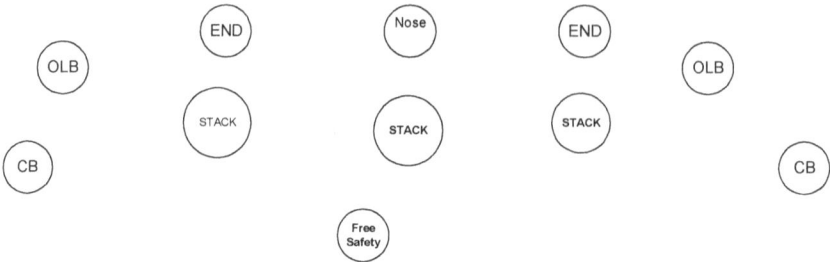

Figure 4. Basic 3-5-3 Defense

LEARN THE POSITIONS

Many teams have different names for the positions in the 3-5-3 defense. It is important to name the positions something that makes sense to your team. For instance, we name our outside linebackers "CUBS" and "BEARS" because our teams at the youth level are "CUBS" and at the high school are the "BEARS." Other teams use the more generic terms of "SPUR" or "DOG" for this position or you can simply call the position "OUTSIDE LINEBACKER."

Defensive Linemen (3)

The defensive linemen play up in the defense. There are three defensive linemen in this defense. There is a nose guard and two defensive ends. The defensive linemen are the first line of defense. The defensive line primarily defends the run and rushes the passer.

Linebackers (5)

The linebackers play behind the line. There are five linebackers in this defense. There are three stack linebackers and two outside linebackers. The stack linebackers can be the mike or middle linebacker, the sam or strong side linebacker and the will or weak side linebacker. The outside linebackers are the cub or left side linebacker and the bear or right side linebacker. The linebackers are the second line of defense. Linebackers must defend the run and the pass.

Defensive Backs (3)

The defensive backs play behind the linebackers. There are 3 defensive backs in this defense. There are two cornerbacks and one free safety. The defensive backs are the third line of defense. Defensive backs prevent passes and runs. The cornerbacks' primary prevent long runs and defend pass plays. In this defense, the free safety must be equal at defending pass plays and playing the run. The free safety is the protection for the pass and the safeguard for linebacker blitzes.

NOTE: In this book, we will use the following for the stack linebacker positions: mike (middle), sam (strong), and will (weak). The outside linebackers are the "Cub" (left) and "Bear" (right). Also, we will use "R" for right corner and "L" for left corner.

COACHING POINT: At the youth and middle school level, it is important to keep it simple. In this defense, you can use sam and will linebackers or you can stack linebackers that do not switch to strong and weak side. We have even switched bear and cub linebackers to have the bear linebacker to the strong side. In addition, we have played cornerbacks to specific field or boundary side of the field. You can do many adjustments depending on your players.

IDENTIFY THE BASIC 3-5-3 BASIC ALIGHNMENT

Figure 5 shows 3-5-3 basic alignment.

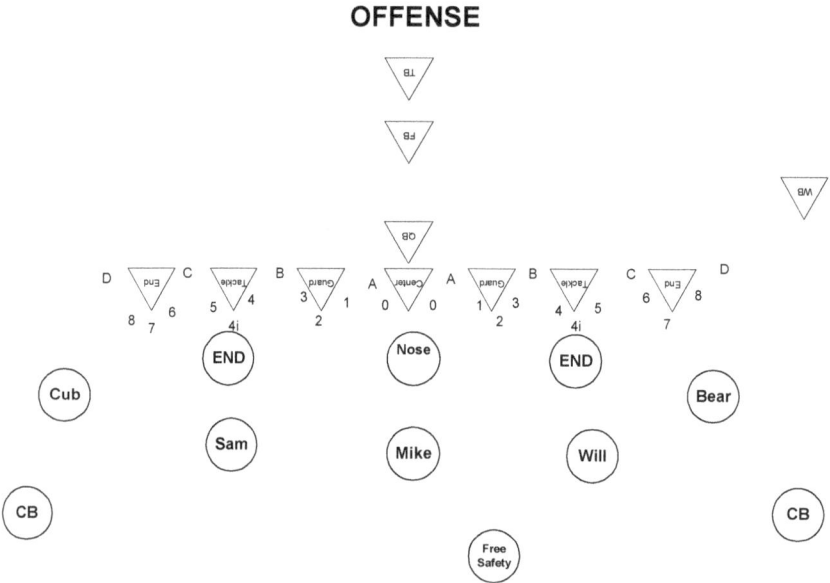

Figure 5.   3-5-3 Basic Alignment

Basic Alignment Defensive Line

- Nose Guard
  - Head up on Center
- Ends
  - Head up on Offensive Tackle

Basic Alignment Linebackers

- Inside Linebackers (Mike, Sam, Will)
  - Stack behind defensive line
- Heels at 2 ½ to 3 yards
  - Outside Linebackers (Bear and Cub)
  - 2 x 2 or 1 x 1 yards from outside line of scrimmage offensive player

Basic Alignment Defensive Backs

- Cornerbacks
  - 1 x 5 yards on #1 receiver on same side
        Inside on Cover 1
        Outside on Cover 3
- Free Safety
  - 1 x 7 yards on strong side (1 yard from center)

GEAR THE BASIC ALIGNMENT TO YOUR TEAM

The table below shows the basic alignment of the 3-5-3 with the adjustments for youth football. When considering the basic alignment for your team, it is important to consider the size, speed and quickness of your defensive players. The coach wants to put the defensive players in position to make plays. For the defensive line, the players line up head-up on the assigned offensive player. For instance, the nose guard lines head-up on the center. For the linebacker and defensive backs at the youth and middle school level, the players are not as big and fast as upper level players. Therefore, generally, the coach will move the linebackers and defensive backs closer to the line of scrimmage.

The following table shows the normal adjustments for youth and middle school football for the 3-5-3 defense.

Youth Alignment Adjustments

Position	Basic Alignment	Adjustments for Youth Football
Strong End	4 eye	Head Up Power (Gap)
Nose	Head-up	Head Up Power (Gap)
End	4 eye	Head Up Power (Gap)
Sam	Stack (heels 5 yards)	Toes at 2 – 2 ½ yards
Mike	Stack (heels at 5 yards)	Toes at 2 – 2 ½ yards
Will	Stack (heels at 5 yards)	Toes at 2 to 2 ½ yards
Cub (LOLB)	3 x 3 yards	1 x 1 LOS (no TE)
Bear (ROLB)	3 x 3	1 x 1 LOS (no TE)
LC	1 x 7	1 x 5
FS	Strong side off Mike 10 – 12 yards	1 x 7 to 1 x 10
RC	1 x 7	1 x 5

Middle School Alignment Adjustments

Position	Basic Alignment	Adjustments for MS Football
Strong End	4 eye	Head Up Power (Gap)
Nose	Head-up	Head Up Power (Gap)
End	4 eye	Head Up Power (Gap)
Sam	Stack (heels 5 yards)	Toes at 2 ½ - 3 –yards
Mike	Stack (heels at 5 yards)	Toes at 2 ½ - 3 yards
Will	Stack (heels at 5 yards)	Toes at 2 ½ to 3 yards
Cub (LOLB)	3 x 3 yards	2 x 2 or 1 x 1 LOS (no TE)
Bear (ROLB)	3 x 3	2 x 2 or 1 x 1 LOS (no TE)
LC	1 x 7	1 x 5
FS	Strong side off Mike 10 – 12 yards	1 x 7 to 1 x 10
RC	1 x 7	1 x 5

The table below shows the basic alignment using a basic numbering system of alignment and adjustment for youth football.

Numbers – Shades on Designated Offensive Lineman	Modified for Youth Football

0 Technique – Shade on the center
 	
1 Technique –Inside shade of offensive guard
 	
2 Technique – Head up on offensive guard
 	
3 Technique – Outside shade on offensive guard
 	
4 Technique – Inside shade on offensive tackle
 	
4 eye Technique – Head up on offensive tackle
 	
5 Technique – Outside shade on offensive tackle
 	
7 Technique –Inside shade on tight end
 	
8 Technique –Head up on tight end
 	
9 Technique – Outside shade on tight end
 	
10 Technique – Area outside of tight end
	Head Up on offensive player
	
	   Nose on Center
	
	   Ends on Tackles
	
	Power
	
	   Line up in the assigned gap

NOMINATE PLAYERS FOR POSITIONS

The general player characteristics for each position in the 3-5-3 defense are determined by your players and your competition. Generally, this is an attacking defense that can use any athlete. In general, we look for the most speed and quickness at every position. You want your defense to be strong up the middle. The nose guard, mike linebacker and free safety need to be your best possible athletics at the position. In youth football, the game sometimes boils down to the fastest on outside runs. This must be a consideration for your players on the outside to include the bear or cub positions and the two corners. In addition to the general characteristics, we will look for certain characteristics for each position depending on the particular competitive situation. For instance, ideally against a run team the nose guard should be the biggest and strongest player. This is not always possible. Therefore, a quick nose guard may be the best option.

Defensive Line

The main responsibilities of the defensive line are: seal the gap, occupy lineman and penetrate into the backfield. It is a plus if the lineman pursues, makes the tackle or sacks the quarterback.

Nose Guard: This player should be the most physically dominating player on the defense. Ideally, this is a dominate defensive lineman that is big and strong. At the youth and middle school level, this type of player is not always available, especially in a weight limitation league. Again, an aggressive, quick player that can disrupt the center and get to the quarterback is effective at this position.

Defensive Tackle(s): The most agile players on the defense. At defensive tackle, mobile and quick players are the most effective. If you have a player with size and quickness, this would be ideal. At the youth and middle school level, we look for linebacker type players at defensive end. At the middle school, we play mostly power running teams. Against this type of team, you might consider more size at the defensive tackles. Speed and quickness is always a plus at this position.

COACHING POINT: Practice all defensive lineman in all three defensive line positions. This allows flexibility to move players to different positions in a game and it also allows rotation of players throughout the game.

Linebackers

Linebackers are the key to this defense. Linebackers are your best athletes on the team. They have gap and pass coverage responsibilities. They also create confusion for the line, make sure tackles and pressure the quarterback. Linebackers play the run first and pass next. For the inside stack linebackers (sam/will) depending on the players, we may or may not switch to strong and weak. At the youth level, you may not want to switch to keep it simple for the players. Some teams also switch outside linebackers (bear/cub) to wide and short sides of the field. As always, you should consider your players as well as the competition.

Stack Linebackers:

Mike: Smartest player on the defense. The mike linebacker is the quarterback of the defense. The mike linebacker needs to be smart and know what everyone is doing on defense.
Sam: Toughest player on the defense
Will: Next toughest linebacker besides the sam linebacker and possibly slowest linebacker on the defense.

Outside linebackers: These players must be combination of linebacker and defensive backs. These are the bear/cub linebackers. The best outside linebacker should be the left (cub) to play against the right side of the offense.

COACHING POINT: Practice all linebackers at all linebacker positions. This allows flexibility to move players to different positions in a game and it also allows rotation of players throughout the game.

Defensive backs: The cornerbacks need to be able to defend the pass as well as make open field tackles. Although passing is becoming more prevalent in youth and middle school football, cornerbacks must be part of the run defense especially at the youth level.

Cornerback: The best cornerback plays the wide side of the field.

Free Safety: The best athlete on the defense. The safety can make up for many mistakes or over aggressiveness.

COACHING POINT: Have the free safety practice with the linebackers during individual sessions of practice as much as possible.

CHAPTER 4
TEACH GAP
RESPONSIBILITIES

TEACH GAP RESPONSIBILITIES

This defense is a gap controlled defense. Every player has gap responsibility. Gap responsibility must be stressed everyday.

Gap designation

Allocate basic gap responsibilities

Practice gap responsibilities everyday

GAP DESIGNATION

Letters designate the gaps for the defense. The gaps are as follows:

A Gap – Area between Offensive Center and Guard

B Gap – Area between Offensive Guard and Tackle

C Gap – Area between Offensive Tackle and TE

D Gap – Area outside of Tight End

On the next page, figure 6 shows the gaps.

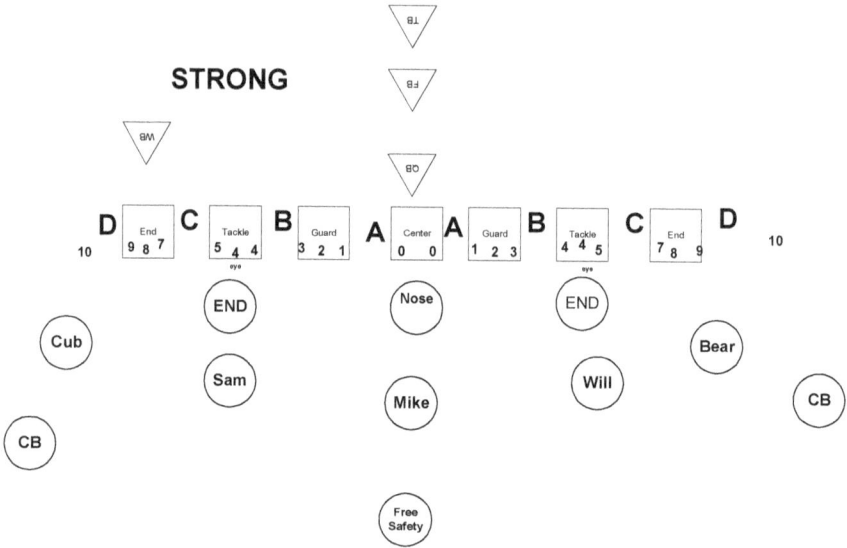

Figure 6. Gap Designation

ALLOCATE BASIC GAP RESPONSIBILITES

The basic gap responsibilities are shown in the table below:

Gap	Responsible
A Gap	Nose Guard Middle Linebacker
B Gap	Defensive Ends Sam/Will Linebackers
C Gap	Defensive Ends Sam/Will Linebacker
D Gap	Bear/Cub
Outside	Bear/Cub Corners

Figure 7 below shows the basic gap responsibilities.

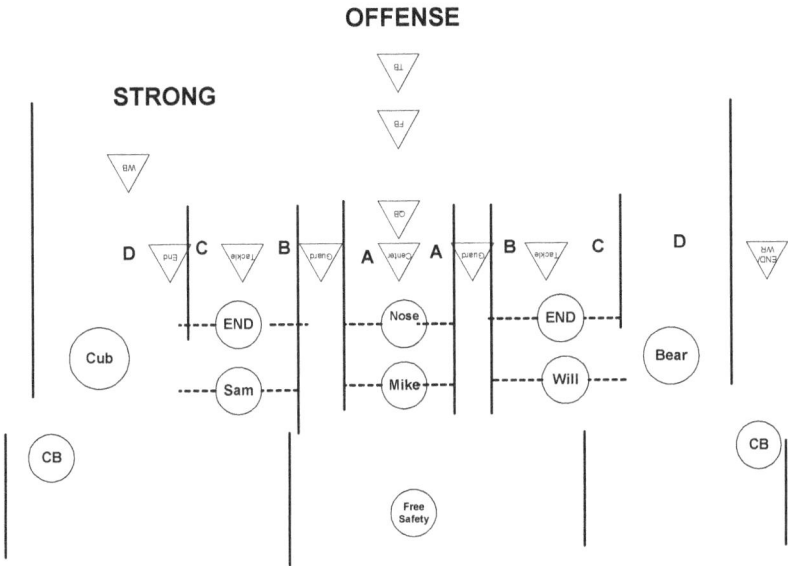

Figure 7. Basic Gap Responsibilities

COACHING POINT: At the youth and middle school level, players are sometimes taught to look for the ball and chase the ball. This defense requires players to attack their specific gap first.

PRACTICE GAP RESPONSIBLIES EVERYDAY

During defensive drills, gap responsibility must be stressed continuously. It is important to do drills with cones, bags or fire hose to simulate gaps. We even have painted offensive players positions on the practice field with gaps designated on the field. This is especially important for the defensive line and the linebackers. The defensive line and linebacker gap responsibilities are shown below.

	DEFENSIVE LINE	**LINEBACKERS**
A GAP	NOSE GUARD	MIKE
B GAP	END	SAM AND WILL
C GAP	END	SAM AND WILL
D GAP		BEAR AND CUB

It is critical to work the gap responsibility with the defensive line and linebackers both individually and together everyday.

On the following pages are two drills for instilling gap responsibilities. One is a drill for defensive line gap responsibilities and the other is a linebacker gap responsibilities drill. These drills can be combined to drill both the linemen and linebackers on gap responsibilities.

Defensive Line Gap Responsibility Drill

All three defensive lineman take their position in front of cone/bag/offensive lineman. The coach calls the play (see chapter 5). The coach uses a ball or ball on a stick to simulate center snap. The defensive line executes the play by stepping to the assigned gap. Figure 8 shows the set-up for the drill.

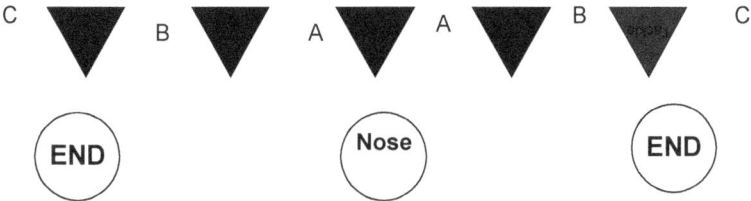

Figure 8. Defensive Line Gap Responsibility Drill

Linebacker Gap Responsibility Drill

All five linebackers take positions in respect to cone/bag/offensive lineman. The coach calls the play (see chapter 5). The coach uses a ball or ball on a stick to simulate center snap. The linebackers execute the play by going into the assigned gap. Blitzer(s) will go though the gap to the cone/running back. Figure 9 shows the set-up for the drill.

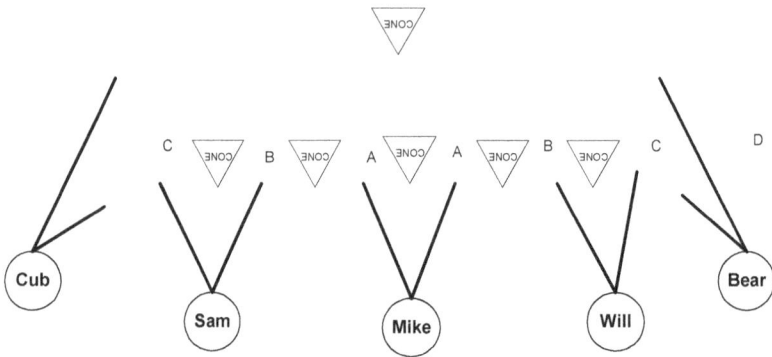

Figure 9. Linebackers Gap Responsibility Drill

COACHING POINT: At the high school and higher levels, players are taught to read keys and react to the play. At the youth and middle school levels, the teams do not always have the typical key reads for the defense. Therefore, this defense at the youth and middle school level should attack the gap and pursue to the ball.

CHAPTER 5
TRAIN FUNDAMENTALS

TRAIN FUNDAMENTALS

Player's performance depends on willingness and ability. It is each coach's responsibility to develop both of these performance factors everyday. At the youth level, it is especially critical to work on the players' willingness factor. The youth player may be participating because of parent(s) or other factor(s). In addition, football is a sport that is different from most sports because of the physical aspects of the sport. The coach must develop confidence in every player to overcome fear of contact.

Besides willingness, the player's ability must be improved everyday. This requires educating and training to develop the knowledge, skills and attitude necessary. There is a difference between educating and training and coaching that must be understood to build a successful defense. Educating focuses on knowledge. Educating involves learning information. Education is always the foundation. Training works on knowledge, skills and attitude to perform a specific task. Coaching is the overall process of striving for excellence for the team and each individual player. This includes planning, preparing, performing and probing. Football requires educating, training and coaching. This chapter will focus on football training.

Train football skills

Recognize required football skills

Apply defensive skills to specific positions

Install 3-5-3 basic play

Numerate progress

TRAIN FOOTBALL SKILLS

Football requires education, involves letting players know about the game of football and football training that targets specific football skills. Football training can be more effective using the following process.

Introduce the football skill

Demonstrate the skill properly

Encourage practice of the skill

Attend to the positive

Let player perform the skill

First, the coach introduces the football skill to the player. It is important to explain the skill in relation to the game of football. The coach should describe the skill step-by-step. Second, the skill must be demonstrated properly by the coach or by another player. It is necessary for coaches to understand that players learn differently. For some players, a simple on-field demonstration is sufficient. Some players can learn from a video. Other players need to be able to try the skill themselves in order to learn the proper technique. Depending on the skills' importance and complexity, the coach should provide several learning methods. Third, it is critical to allow the player to practice the skill. Many football skills require repeated repetition of fundamental skills. At the youth level, it is critical to develop good habits. Fourth, the coach must focus on the positive aspect of the player's skill development. In addition, the coach needs to take corrective action to ensure proper execution of the skill. The coach provides feedback on the positive and negative performance of the skill. It might be appropriate to provide another proper demonstration. The coach should always try to finish the feedback with a word of encouragement. Fifth, the player must be allowed to perform the skill in a game-like situation.

COACHING POINT: Make it a coaching rule to never let a player perform a skill in a game that he/she did not have a chance to practice perfect.

RECONGIZE FOOTBALL SKILLS

The first step in football training is to determine the basic skills. For youth and middle school football, it is important to recognize the fundamentals for each position. The football skills should progress from the individual skill, to the position skill, to the team.

COACHING POINT: Coaches must remember the age and skill level of the players. Many coaches expect performance from youth players beyond their years.

All Defense Skills

The following fundamental skills are required for every player on the defense. These fundamental skills should be practiced perfect at every practice. These skills are:
- Stance
- Movement
- Defeat the Blocker
- Tackling

Specific Defense Skills by Position

Defensive Line
- Stance
- Movement
- Step and rip
- Tackling
- Fumble recovery (drop and cover)

> Pass rush

Inside Linebacker
> Stance
> Movement
> Defeat Blocker
> Tackling
> Pursuit
> Ball Strip
> Fumble recovery (scoop and score)
> Pass interception
> Pass coverage

Outside Linebacker
> Stance
> Movement
> Defeat blocker
> Tackling
> Pursuit
> Ball Strip
> Fumble recovery (scoop and score)
> Pass interception
> Pass coverage

Cornerbacks
> Stance
> Movement
> Tackling
> Pass Coverage
  - Man-to-Man
  - Zone
> Pass Interception

Safety
> Stance
> Movement

> Tackling
> Pass Interception
> Pass Coverage

APPLY DEFENSE SKILLS TO SPECIFIC POSITIONS

It is important for each defensive player to practice perfect specific skills for his/her position. For youth and middle school players, coaches must keep it simple.

COACHING POINT: Coaches must integrate the following fundamentals into every defensive practice: stance, movement, defeat the blocker, and tackling.

Fundamentals for Defensive Line

Defensive linemen's roles are:

> to maintain specific gap responsibility
> to penetrate into the backfield
> to stop the run
> to rush the passer

These roles and responsibilities must be constantly in mind when teaching fundamental skills. Above all else, the number one rule is to maintain gap responsibility. Defensive linemen perform their job if they fill gaps and occupy offensive lineman.

Stance

In the 3-5-3 defense, players can use the three-point, four-point or two-point stances. The specific stance depends on the player. Since everything starts with the stance, the player must be comfortable in the stance. We always start with the basic balanced three-point stance. The steps for the three-point stance are described below. The two-point stance has been successful for the defensive ends. For the defensive lineman, the two-point stance is basically the three-point stance without putting the hand down. On occasion, the nose guard can benefit from using a four point stance. With the four-point stance, the lineman puts both hands down, gets low and put more weight out front.

Three Point Stance Defensive Lineman Instruction

- Stand straight up with feet together
- Move feet out even to the hip width or slightly wider
- Keep toes pointed straight ahead
- Bend knees so forearms rest on inside of thighs
- Reach straight out with hand right or left hand (right or left handed)
- Place hand on ground slightly (three fingers) ahead of shoulder pads
- Keep shoulders even with back straight
- Have weight on hand and balls of feet
- Keep head up and eyes straight ahead

COACHING POINT: For this defense, the defensive lineman must go equal to right or left. Therefore, a balanced stance is recommended. However, a player may put the dominate foot back slightly, if it helps the player.

Two Point Stance Defensive Lineman Instruction

- Feet are shoulder width apart or slightly wider
- Toes pointed straight forward (balanced or one foot slightly back)
- Weight of body on toes and balls of the feet
- Knees bent and positioned slightly beyond feet (get low)
- Legs tense and ready to take sudden movement
- Hands positioned slightly outside knee joint with palms facing inward and parallel to leg

- Neck bulled with eyes looking up at the target
- Upper body relaxed in order to move quickly

Movement

The movement for defensive lineman in the 3-5-3 defense is simple. They will lineup head-up on the offensive lineman and they will move either right or left into the assigned gap. They must first penetrate and then pursue. They step toward the gap and rip past the lineman as quickly as possible and pursue the ball-carrier. At the youth and middle school level, the step and rip is the only technique required for effective defensive line play in the 3-5-3 defense.

Movement Instruction

- Step toward the assigned gap with the foot at the gap
- Do not take a false step with away foot
- Aim for hip of offense player that is not head up
- Make sure you make penetration with initial step
- Rip across offensive player in front of you

COACHING POINT: Defensive lineman must always get off on the ball. Coaches make sure all movement drills use ball movement and not whistle or voice. Coaches have the nose guard watch the hand of the center and/or quarterback. The center or quarterback might display an indicator to get a jump on the snap.

Pursuit

Proper pursuit is critical to defensive line play. The best instruction for pursuit involves calling defensive plays against some form of skeleton offense. The defensive line must pursue against the run and pass.

Tackling

At any level of football, tackling is one of the basic skills required for a good defense. At the youth level and some degree at the middle school, teaching tackling is a challenge. Tackling practice causes many injuries and many players are afraid to tackle. The youth coach must be aware of the challenges by building confidence in the players and teaching proper technique. Also, coaches should understand that each player gets the "AHA" of tackling differently. Some players are naturals and other players require some time to learn and gain confidence.

During all tackling drills, the following rules are recommended:

- Safety first – most injuries occur during tackling practice
- Keep players a close physical match
- Keep tackling within 5 yards
- Stress technique (head up and rotate hips)
- **NO**
    - Bull in the ring (excessive injuries)
    - On back head-on-head (promotes head down tackling)
    - Open field tackling over 10 yards (not necessary)

COACHING POINT: Many coaches think tackling is a matter of toughness. Therefore, the first thing they want to do is see how tough the players are by doing one or more of the NO drills above. We believe at the younger level tackling is a combination of confidence and technique. They learn the proper technique and they build confidence to perform the skill by repetition.

There are many types of tackling on the football field. These types are: head-on, angle, open field, sideline, gang tackling, goal line and just get the player down. A head-on tackle happens when the ball-carrier is coming straight at the defensive player. An angle tackle is when the ball-carrier is not directly in front of the defensive player. This is the most predominate type of tackle. An open field tackle is necessary when the defensive player must make a sure one-on-one tackle on the ball-carrier. A sideline tackle is when the ball-carrier is running close to the sideline. Gang tackling is when more than one player makes the tackle. Goal line or short yardage tackling is when the defensive player must prevent the ball-carrier from getting a short gain for a touchdown or first down. Finally, every player must understand in a game, he/she must use any legal method to get the ball-carrier down.

All defensive players should be taught all the different tackling types. However, the types of tackling a position is most likely to perform must be practiced every defensive practice. Defensive linemen mostly tackle within the box of the ends. These tackles are mostly angle tackles with some head-on tackles. Therefore, most tackling practice for defensive lineman should be head-on and angle tackles. Also, they should do goal line or short yardage tackling.

Tackling Basic Instructions

- Hit the ball-carrier first
- Stay low in football position
- Head up – eyes to the sky
- Rotate the hips
- Make contact and wrap (grab)
  - Waist
  - Chest
- Drive through the ball carrier and take backwards

COACHING POINT: At the youth and middle school level, head up tackling must be stressed to avoid injuries. We recommend teaching both waist (low) and chest (high) tackling techniques. The high tackling technique works best for teaching proper technique.

Tackling Progression Instructions

Tackle Preparation
Defensive Player (DP) and Offensive Player (OP) knell facing each other about 12 inches apart
DP leans back on heels
OP gives a forward lean
On command, the DP launches forward, eyes to the sky, rotate hips and wrap (waist and chest)
Standing Tackle - Do above from a standing position.
Form tackle
FIT: The coach has the DP and RB face each other 6 inches apart. DP is fitted to RB in proper contact position. DP knees bent and hips lowered and back straight and head up. His eyes focused on numbers (chest) of RB.
FIT AND LIFT: On command the designated defenders walk up to their partner and into a good fit position. On the next command they follow through, rolling their hips and lifting their partner and taking him back a few steps.
FORM TACKLING: Partners should be about 5 yards apart. On command the designated offender jogs toward the defender. The defender meets him in proper tackling position and performs a form tackle. Have offenders jog in a 45° angle also. Use left and right shoulder.
Three Whistle Drill
Whistle one: step into **HIT** position (football position)
Whistle two: **WRAP**
Whistle three: lift and **DRIVE**

Mat Tackling
    Head on
    Angle
End of Bag Tackling
    Head on
    Angle
5 yard End of Bag Tackling
    Head on
    Angle
Shed and Tackle
Open Field Tackling
Sideline Tackling
Goal line Tackling

COACHING POINT: During practice the coach should have players tackle other players as much as possible. This allows players to experience the feel of proper tackling. Tackling dummies promotes head down tendencies.

Head On Tackling Instruction

- Get under control (football position)
- Keep head up, bend knees to stay low with eyes on ball-carrier
- Aim for the middle lower part of the chest (high) or belt buckle on waist (low)
- Hit with chest (high) or front part of shoulder (low) using same foot to drive
- Put eyes on v of neck (high) or mid-section of ball-carrier (low)
- Wrap arms around ball-carrier and squeeze
- Rotate hips to force ball-carrier back while hitting through the ball-carrier
- Grab hold of the ball-carrier (jersey (high) or back of upper leg right below buttocks)
- Keep feet moving as fast as possible (running)

Angle Tackling Instruction

- Get in under control (football position)
- Keep head up, bend knees to stay low with eyes on ball-carrier
- Aim for the middle lower part of the chest (high) or belt buckle on waist (low)
- Hit with chest (high) or front part of shoulder (low) using same foot to drive
- Ensure body in front of ball-carrier
- Put head to side of ball-carrier's shoulder (high)
- Place eyes (facemask) on the ball or try to put facemask in the bicep (low)
- Wrap arms around ball-carrier at same level and squeeze
- Rotate hips to force ball-carrier back while hitting through the ball-carrier
- Grab hold of the ball-carrier (jersey (high) or back of upper leg right below buttocks)
- Keep feet moving as fast as possible (running)

Goal Line Tackling

For goal line tackling, the players must use the same technique as head-on or angle tackling. The only difference for goal line tackling is to stress the low tackle.

Fundamentals for Linebackers

Linebackers are the heart of a great 3-5-3 defense. Linebackers must win battles on every play. Linebackers' roles are:
- ➤ Confuse the offense
- ➤ Stop the run
- ➤ Contain outside run
- ➤ Prevent pass

Linebacker Stance

Two Point Stack Linebackers Stance Instructions

- Two point, feet about shoulder width apart
- Angles in your ankles, knees and hips
- Grip the grass with your toes, weight on balls of feet
- Head up, big chest
- Arms relaxed on front of you

Two Point Outside Linebackers Stance Instructions

- Two point, feet about shoulder width apart
- Place outside foot back at an angle
- Angles in your ankles, knees and hips
- Grip the grass with your toes, weight on balls of feet
- Head up, turn eyes inside
- Arms relaxed at your sides

Football Stance

Every player needs to learn the football stance. The football stance is the fundamental position for both offensive players and defensive players getting ready to make specific plays on the football field. For defensive players, the football position is the position for getting ready to defeat a blocker and make a tackle. The football stance is similar to the inside linebacker stance.

Football Position Instruction

- Feet shoulder width apart or slightly wider
- Toes pointed straight forward
- Weight of body on toes and balls of the feet
- Knees bent and positioned slightly beyond feet
- Legs tense and ready to take sudden movement
- Hands positioned slightly outside knee joint with palms facing inward and parallel to leg
- Neck bulled with eyes looking up at the target
- Lower back has reverse arc
- Upper body ready to move quickly

COACHING POINT: The football stance is sometimes called the breakdown. Players on defense should breakdown when getting ready to make a play.

Movement

Linebackers must attack. A linebackers first movement should be a small step to attack his/her gap. Linebackers must get in position to make a play. Blitzing linebackers run through the gap as fast as possible staying low with head up.
- Gap step
- Stay square to LOS (Line of scrimmage)
- ATTACK – must get into the LOS

- Cannot get blocked – shed blockers
- Make things happen, pursue the football

Outside linebacker movement

- Read step
- ATTACK – must get into the LOS
- Cannot get blocked – shed blockers
- Make things happen, pursue the football

COACHING POINT: At the youth and middle school level, we stress aggressive play by the linebackers. Especially at the youth level, we emphasize gap responsibility. We do not even introduce offensive play keys. At the middle school level, keys are introduced to the linebackers before the season and they are reviewed during the season. Keys are then used for specific situations.

Pursuit

Proper pursuit is critical to linebacker play in this defense. This skill must have a place in practice. The player must understand proper pursuit angles. The best instruction for pursuit involves calling defensive plays against a some form of skeleton offense.

COACHING POINT: Pursuit drills using chutes allows the linebackers to practice proper stance, movement and pursuit.

Defeat the Blocker

Linebackers need to be able to defeat blockers quickly. Again, youth players need it simple. The major weapon for linebackers to defeat the blocker in this defense is using the stun technique.

Stun Instructions

- Key movement to blocker (eyes fixed)
- Strike with same foot – same shoulder
- Strike pad under pad – work through the V of the neck
- Aim to put your nose on the V of the neck to maintain gap control
- Have great timing to deliver a blow
- Punch and release
- Hands
  - Punch with the heel of the hands with the thumbs up and elbows in
  - Aim for chest around shoulder pad front
  - Hit as quickly as possible to shock the block (boxer)
- Feet
  - At contact dip (knee bend) and come out of your shoes
- Accelerate your feet for balance
- Assume football position
- Pursue

Stun and Shed Instructions

- Stun as above
- Shed (if stun itself does not work)
  - Keep gap responsibility (Keep outside leverage)
  - Grab and throw opposite your gap responsibility

Outside Linebacker Defeat the Blocker

The outside linebackers must maintain containment. This means they must always try to turn the running back toward the inside.

Stun Outside Linebacker

- Keep outside position
- Attack outside half of the blocker
- Strike with same foot – same shoulder
- Strike pad under pad – work through the V of the neck
- Have great timing to deliver a blow
- Punch and release
- Assume football position
- Pursue

COACHING POINT: Ideally, the offensive line will be so confused that linebackers will not have to defeat blockers. However, when a linebacker encounters a blocker they must defeat the blocker quick. There is no time for complex techniques.

Tackling

Linebacker should make the most tackles in this defense. Linebackers must win the battle on every play. They must use proper tackling technique (see basic tackling instructions under defensive lineman tackling). Linebackers must pursue and punish. Linebackers must be proficient in head-on and angle tackling. In addition, they must be excellent open field tacklers.

Open Field Tackling Instruction

- Get under control (football position)
- Keep head up, bend knees to stay low with eyes on ball-carrier
- Aim for the middle lower part of the chest (high) or belt buckle on waist (low)
- Hit with chest (high) or front part of shoulder (low) using same foot to drive
- Ensure body in front of ball-carrier
- Put head to side of ball-carrier's shoulder (high)
- Place eyes (facemask) on the ball or try to get facemask on the bicep (low)
- Wrap arms around ball-carrier at same level and squeeze
- Grab hold of the ball-carrier (jersey (high) or back of upper leg right below buttocks)
- Keep feet moving
- Keep control of ball-carrier, take to ground or hold for help

Pass Coverage Techniques

General Cover Instructions

- Recognize down and distance
- Recognize pass keys
- Recognize formation/patterns in zone coverage
- See QB in zone
- Recognize correct man and play tough man coverage

Pass Defense Instructions

- Pre-snap: Check down and distance, formation and landmarks

- Keys
  - Near back pass sets
  - QB high ball
  - Guard has high hat
- Pass Reaction
- Read routes early QB late

- Zone Instructions
  - Sprint to landmarks and square up
  - Hook/Curl – 12 to 15 yards deep on hash
  - Soft – 12 -15 yards deep, split uprights in middle of field
  - Break on QB indicators

- Man to Man Instructions
  - Concentrate on your man
  - Establish inside leverage and wall receiver to the outside
  - Read receiver's hips for breaks
  - Do not look back at QB, read receivers hands and eyes as an indicator for the ball

- Play Action Pass Instructions
  - Honor a "good" play fake – look for a tip from lineman or QB
  - Work for depth between the nearest receiver and QB
  - Go to pass coverage responsibility zone or man

Fundamentals for Defensive Backs

Cornerbacks' primary responsibility is the pass. In youth and middle school football, they are also key players to stop outside runs.

Stance

The stance for cornerbacks is two-point.

Two Point Stance Cornerback Instructions

- Upper body relaxed to move quickly
- Feet shoulder width, then put outside foot forward (zone), inside foot forward (man-to-man) (split the defender in half)
- Bring foot forward and in, until lined up directly under the chin
- Toes pointed straight forward
- Knees bent slightly
- Weight on the front foot
- Head up, tilted slightly in the inside looking at the ball

Two-Point Stance Free Safety

- Upper body relaxed to move quickly
- Feet shoulder width
- Put dominate foot back slightly
- Toes pointed straight forward
- Knees bent slightly
- Weight on the front foot
- Head up, tilted slightly in the inside looking at the ball

Movement

The cornerback's first movement is backpedal three steps to read pass or run. The free safety takes two steps backwards to read the play.

Defeat the Blocker

For the defensive backs the stun and stun and shed techniques are the primary method to defeat the blocker. In addition, defensive backs can usually just outrun or out maneuver the blocker.

Tackling

Defensive backs must be competent open field and sideline tacklers. See basic tackling instructions under defensive lineman tackling and open field tackling under linebacker's tackling.

Sideline Tackling Instructions

- Get in under control (football position)
- Keep head up, bend knees to stay low with eyes on ball-carrier
- Position yourself so the ball-carrier must either run into you or out-of-bounds.
- Take away the cutback
- Hit the ball-carrier to drive (or push) the ball-carrier out-of-bounds

Pass Coverage

General Cover Instructions

- Recognize down and distance
- Recognize pass keys
- Recognize formation/patterns in zone coverage
- See QB in zone
- Recognize correct man and play tough man coverage

Pass Defense Instructions

- Pre-snap: Check down and distance, formation and landmarks
- Keys
  - QB high ball
  - Guard has high hat
  - Receiver play
- Pass Reaction
- Read routes early QB late

- Zone Instructions
  - Line up outside half on receiver
  - Sprint to landmarks and square up
  - Cornerbacks outside 1/3
  - Free Safety Middle 1/3
  - Break on Receiver/QB indicators

- Man to Man Instructions
  - Line up inside half on receiver
  - Concentrate on your man
  - Read receiver's hips for breaks
  - Do not look back at QB, read receivers hands and eyes as an indicator for the ball

Pass Interception

- Make sure you can make the play
- Try to catch ball at highest point
- Catch, tuck and yell "bingo"

INSTALL 3-5-3 PLAY

Installing 3-5-3 play involves the stunts for the defensive line and various blitzes for linebackers, corners and free safety. Every play in the 3-5-3 involves a stunt by the defensive line and at least one blitz.

3-5-3 Defensive Line Play

Defensive line play for the 3-5-3 defense involves two basic movements. These movements are to the right and to the left. For the defensive ends, this is movement to "B" gap or the "C" gap. The defensive ends can each go to the "C" gap. We call this "stack." This is also called "open" or "out." The defensive ends can both go to "B" gap. We call this "pinch." This is also called "close" or "in." The defensive ends can also both go to the strong side. We call this "slant." The defensive ends can also go to the weak side. We call this "angle." At the youth and middle school level, these four plays for the defensive line are enough for most situations. The only other adjustment is "power." Power means that the defensive line lines up in the assigned gap.

For the nose guard, this is movement to "A" gap to the strong side or weak side. We call this "strong" and "weak."

These movements are shown in the following three pages. Again the defensive end stunts are:
- Stack
- Pinch
- Slant
- Angle

The nose guard stunts are:
- Strong
- Weak

Defensive End Stunt Stack (Outside)

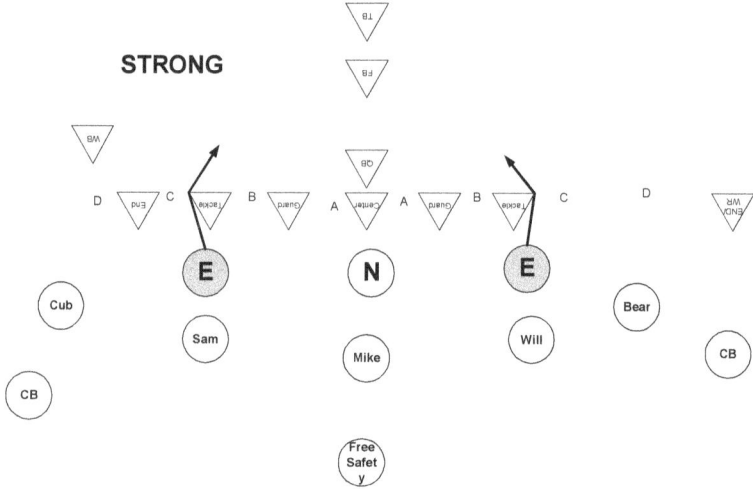

Defensive End Stunt Pinch (Inside)

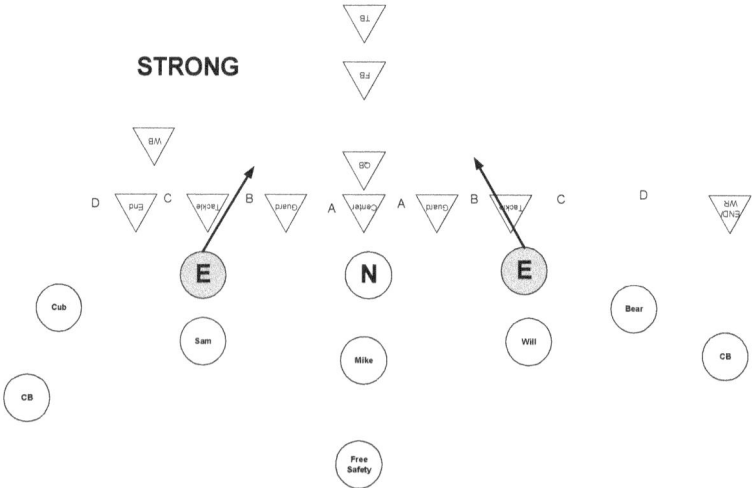

Defensive End Stunt Slant (Strong)

Defensive End Stunt Angle (Weak)

Nose Guard Stunt Strong

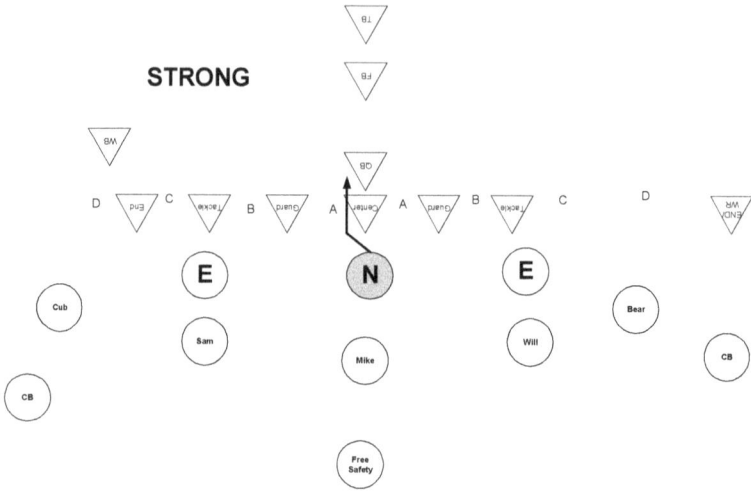

STRONG

Nose Guard Stunt Weak

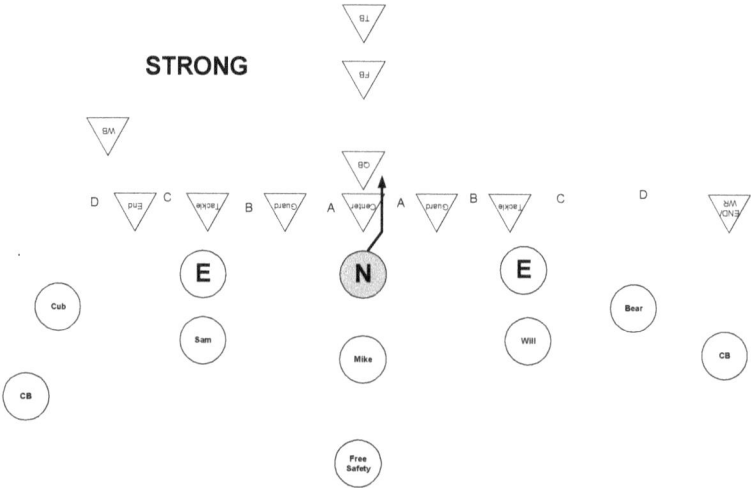

STRONG

Linebacker Blitz

The defensive line and the linebackers work together to ensure all the gaps in the defense are filled by gap assignment. The defensive stunts and the linebacker blitzes must fill all gap responsibilities. Linebacker blitzes are coordinated with the defensive line stunts in the 3-5-3 defense. The nose guard and the mike linebacker both have the "A" gap. The defensive ends and the stack linebackers have the "B" and "C" gaps. Therefore, the nose guard stunt to the strong side must have the mike linebacker filling the weak (away) gap or blitzing through the weak side "A" gap.

    The table below shows the blitzes by linebackers. The mike linebacker can blitz through the "A" gap. We call this the "Ace" blitz. The mike linebacker can blitz "TO" the strong side "A" gap or "AWAY" from the strong side "A" gap. The sam or will can blitz to the "B" gap. We call this the "Bang" blitz. The sam can blitz "TO" the strong side "B" gap. The will can blitz "AWAY" from the strong side "B" gap. We call "Bang" for the sam and will both to blitz their "B" gap. In addition the sam or will can blitz the "C" gap. We call this the "Crack" blitz. The sam can blitz the "TO" the strong side "C" gap and the will can blitz "AWAY" from the strong side "C" gap. We call "Crack" for both the sam and will to blitz their "C" gap. The bear and cub can blitz the "D" gap. The "D" gap blitz to the strong side by the outside linebacker is call lightning "TO" and the "D" gap blitz away for the strong side is called lightning "AWAY." We call the blitz for both the bear and cub linebackers to blitz just "Lightning."

    The figures over the next pages show the blitzes.

Linebacker	Gap	Call	Blitz
Mike	A	Ace	TO or AWAY
Sam/Will	B	Bang	TO or AWAY or Bang (both)
Sam/Will	C	Crack	TO or AWAY or Crack (both)
Bear/Cub	D	Lightning	TO or AWAY or Lightning (both)

COACHING POINT: The blitz calls are simple. The blitz call is "To" or "Away" from the strong side call. The blitz call without the "To" or "Away" means both linebackers blitz.

Mike Linebacker Blitz - MIKE ACE TO

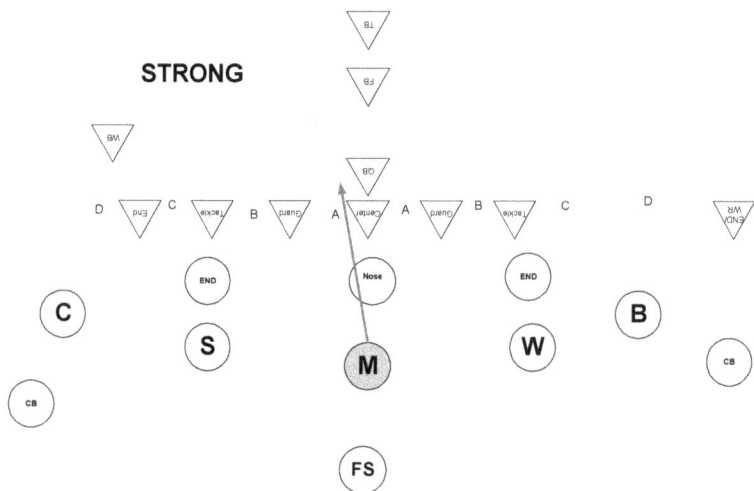

Mike Linebacker Blitz - MIKE ACE AWAY

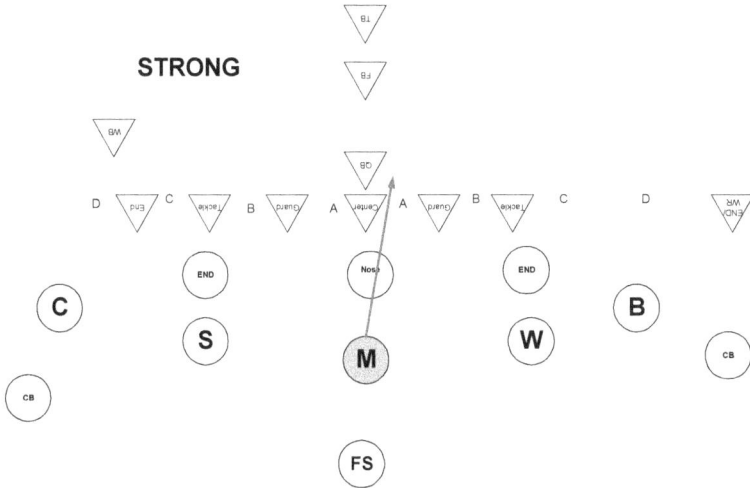

Sam Linebacker BANG TO

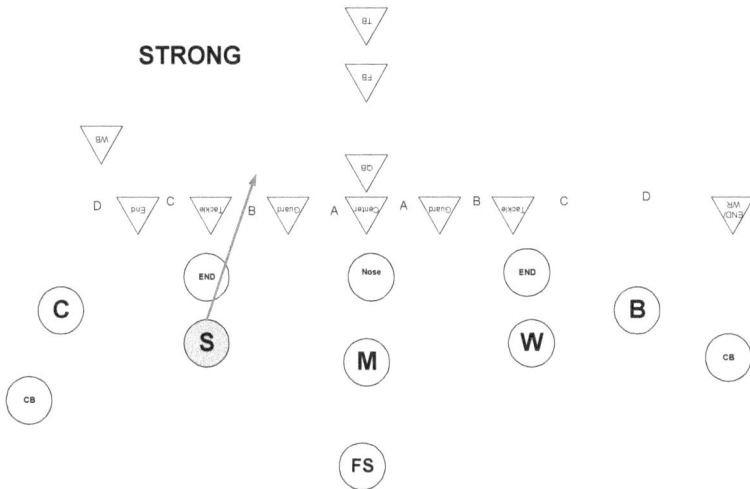

Sam Linebacker CRACK TO

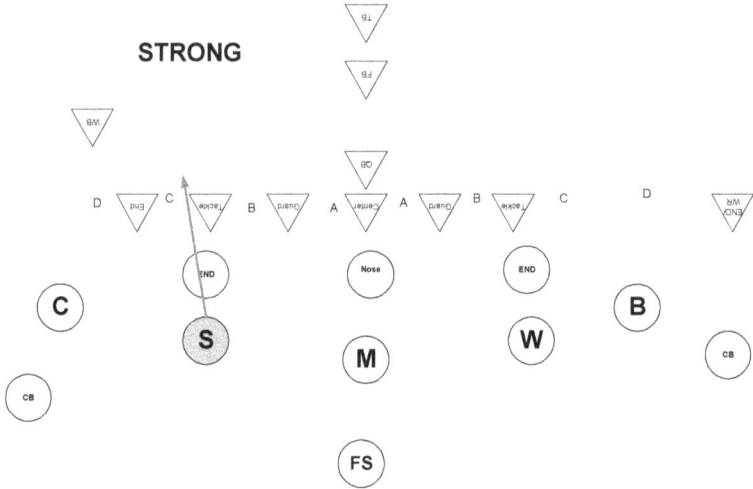

Will Linebacker BANG AWAY

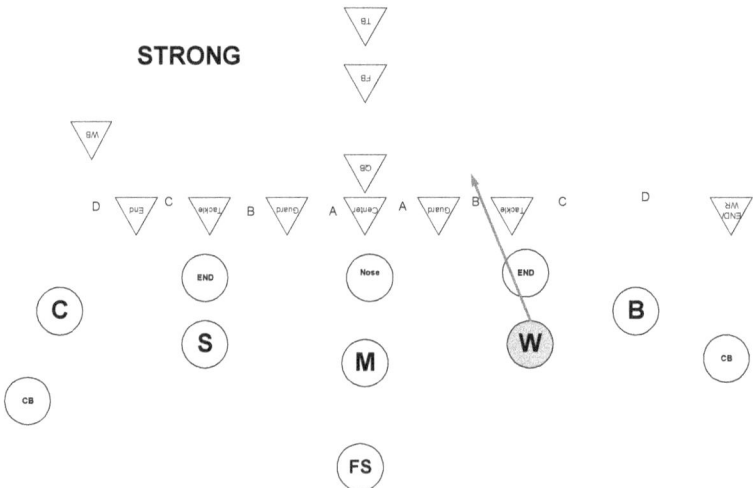

Will Linebacker CRACK AWAY

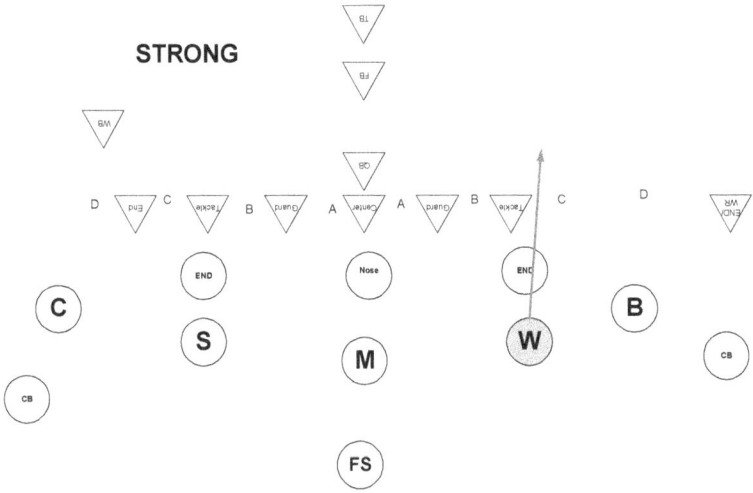

Sam and Will Linebackers BANG

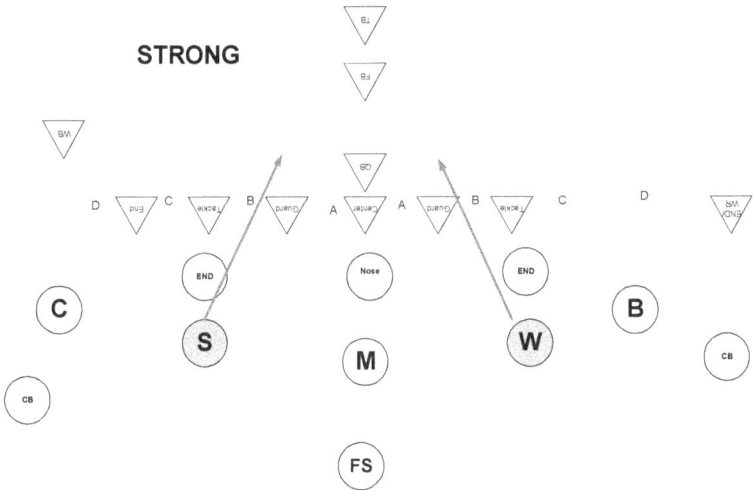

Sam and Will Linebackers CRACK

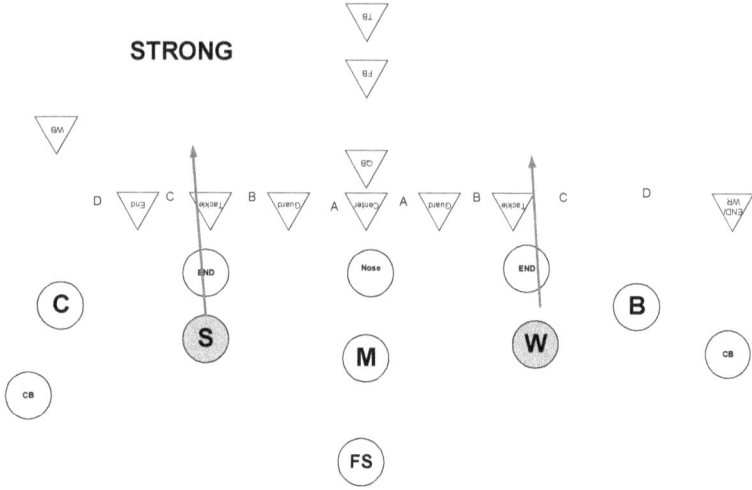

Outside Linebacker (BEAR OR CUB) LIGTHNING TO

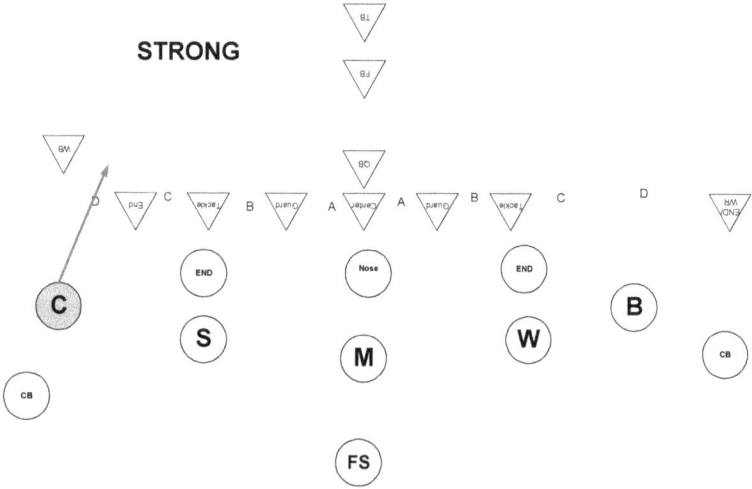

Outside Linebacker (BEAR OR CUB) LIGHTNING AWAY)

STRONG

OLB (BEAR AND CUB) LIGHTNING

STRONG

Defensive Backs Blitz

The defensive backs blitzes are:

> Cornerback
> > Smoke To and Away
> > Smoke
>
> Free Safety
> > Blast To and Away
> > Blast

The cornerback blitz "smoke to" is the strong side cornerback blitz. The cornerback "smoke away" blitz is the weak side cornerback blitz. The "smoke" blitz is both the cornerbacks blitzing.

The safety blitz "blast to" is the strong side blitz. The safety "blast away" blitz is the weak side blitz. The safety "blast" blitz is the middle "A" gap blitz by the safety.

Corner Back Blitz SMOKE TO

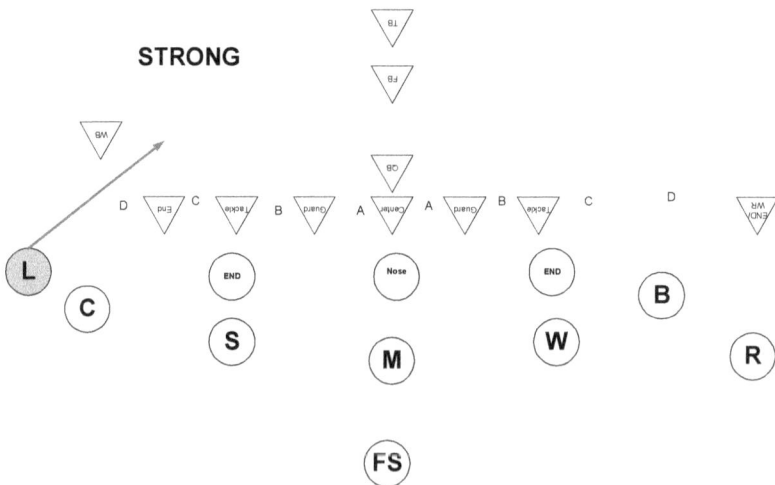

Corner Back Blitz SMOKE AWAY

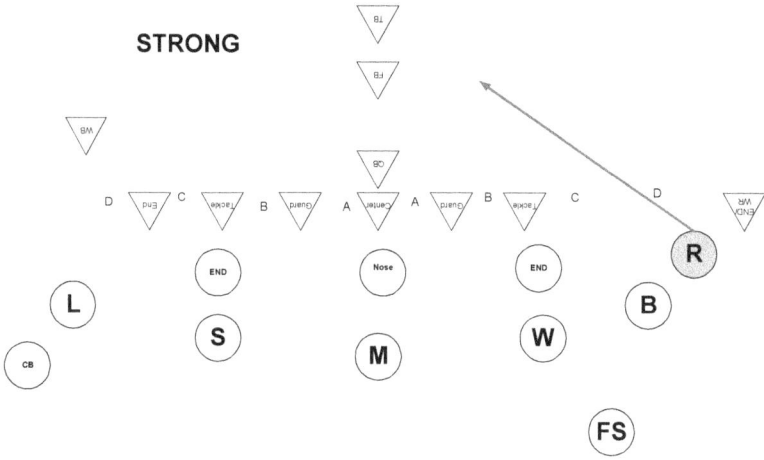

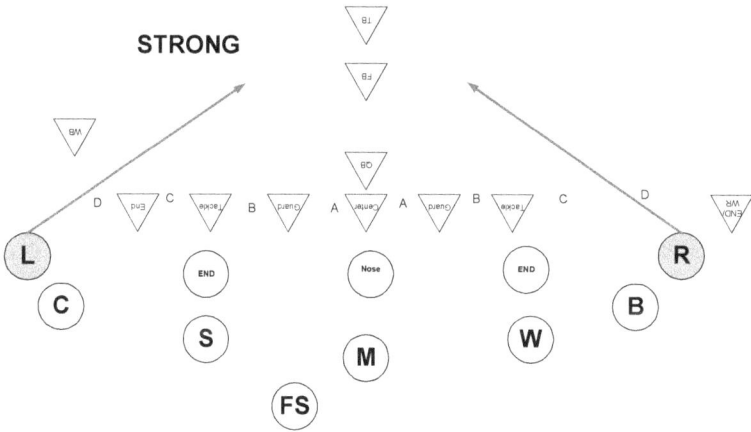

STRONG

Corner Back Blitz SMOKE

STRONG

3-5-3 Defense

Free Safety BLAST TO

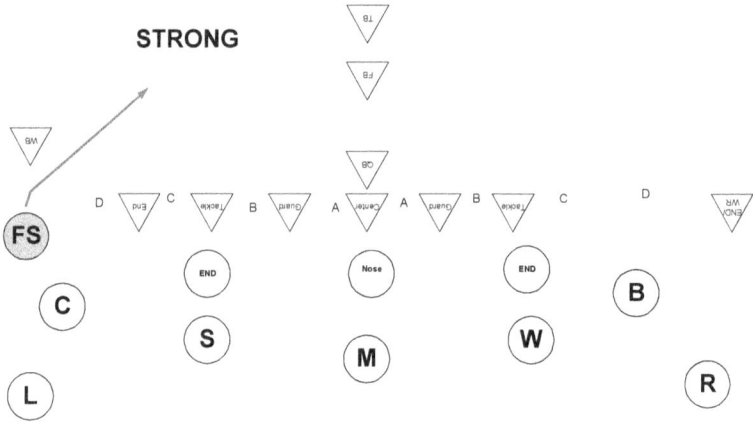

STRONG

Free Safety BLAST AWAY

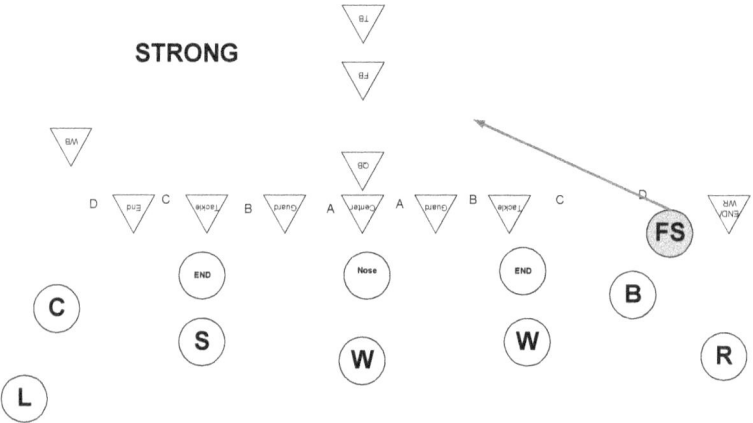

STRONG

Free Safety BLAST

Pass Coverage

In this defense for the youth and middle school, we recommend using only cover 1 (man-to-man with free safety) and cover 3 (zone) coverage. These two coverages are effective for most situations. For special situations, the free safety will not be free (cover 0).

COACHING POINT: At the youth level, the coach needs to determine if they should use cover 1 or cover 3 or both coverages. For some teams, cover 1 may be easiest to teach and for other teams cover 3 may be the best. At the middle school, we have been successful using both cover 1 and cover 3 coverages.

Cover 1 – Man Coverage

Cover 1 is man-to-man coverage with a free safety. In this coverage, this is man free safety coverage. We will look underneath and keep the free safety free over the top. We will blitz linebackers and apply pressure to the QB. The free safety is free. The one basic exception to the free safety is when there is trips. In this case, the free safety locks on #3 on trips side.

COACHING POINT: For the youth and middle school team, keep the coverage simple. The CB always have the #1 receiver on the outside. The OLB always has the #2 receiver. Therefore, the only decision is the #3 or #4 receiver. The defense does not adjust for motion. It is always the count from the boundary in of eligible receivers.

Figure 10 below shows typical cover 1 man coverage.

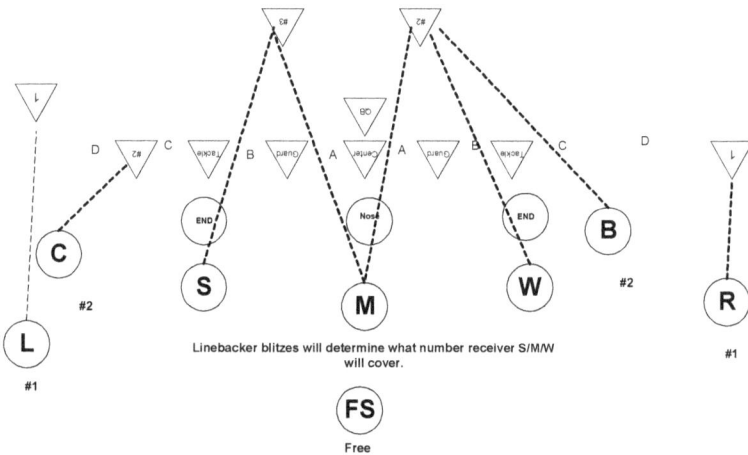

Linebacker blitzes will determine what number receiver S/M/W will cover.

Figure 10. Man-to-Man Coverage - Cover 1.

The tables below outlines man-to-man responsibilities.

Player	Alignment	Key	Pass
Corner	1 x 5 - 7 inside	#1	M/M on #1
Free Safety	Strong side 7 - 10 yards	LOS Ball/#2	Free
Corner	1 x 5- 7 inside	#1	M/M on #1
Cub	2 x 2 vs TE split difference vs twins	#2	M/M on #2
Bear	1 x 1 vs no TE split difference vs twins	#2	M/M on #2
Sam/Will	Stack	#3	M/M on # 3
Mike	Stack	Help #3	M/M help on #3

Cover 3 – Zone Coverage

This is our 3-deep and 5 under zone package. The number of under will change depending on the blitz package. If we blitz 1 linebacker, the under will be 4 man. If we blitz 2 linebackers, the under will be 3 man. This coverage gives best run support and is very good against the big play. No team should ever get more than 25 yards against this coverage. In this defense no one gets behind the deep coverage.

Figure 11 below shows the coverage for cover 3 zone.

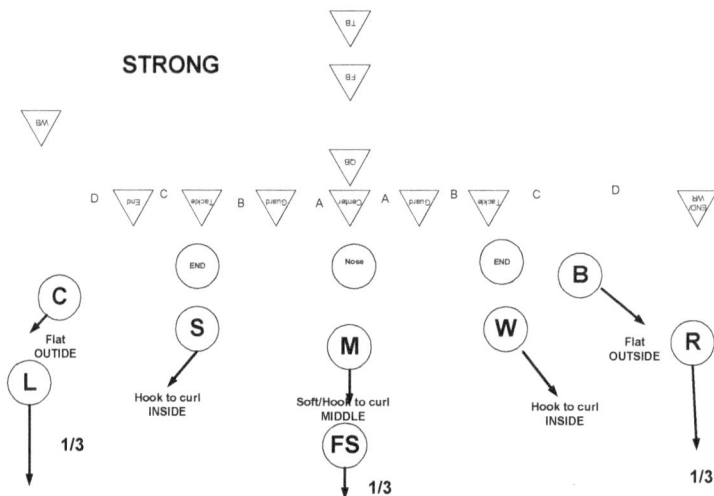

Figure 11. Zone Coverage - Cover 3.

The tables below outlines zone cover 3 responsibilities

Player	Alignment	Key	Pass
Corner	1 x 5 7 outside	Ball/#1	Deep outside 1/3
Free Safety	Strong side 7 - 10 yards	LOS Ball/#2	Deep Middle 1/3
Corner	1 x 5 -7 outside	Ball/#1	Deep outside 1/3
Cub	2 x 2 vs TE split difference vs twins	Triangle OL/NB/Ball	OUTSIDE Flat 12 – 14 yards
Bear	1 x 1 vs no TE split difference vs twins	Triangle OL/NB/Ball	OUTSIDE Flat 12 – 14 yards
Sam/Will	Stack	G/NB/Ball	INSIDE Hook to curl 12 – 14 yards
Mike	Stack	G/NB/Ball	MIDDLE Soft/ Hook to curl 12 – 14 yards

Blitz Adjustments Man-to Man Cover 1

One player blitz – Man-to Man Cover 1

Blitz	Blitzer	Adjustment
Ace	Mike	Open
Bang	Sam/Will	Mike replaces blitzer
Crack	Sam/Will	Mike replaces blitzer
Lighting	Bear/Cub	Sam/Will replace blitzer
Smoke	Cornerback	Free Safety replaces blitzer
Blast	Free Safety	Open

Blitz Adjustments – Zone Cover 3

In the 3-5-3 defense, there is always at least one linebacker blitzing on every play.

One player blitz zone Cover 3

With a one man blitz, the coverage is four linebackers under and 3 defensive backs over. In this coverage, short middle zone is open.

Table one man blitz Cover 3 zone

Blitz	Blitzer	Adjustment
Ace To or Away	Mike	Open
Bang To or Away	Sam/Will	Mike takes place of blitzer (INSIDE)
Crack To or Away	Sam/Will	Mike takes place of blitzer (INSIDE)
Lightning To or Away	Bear/Cub	Sam/Will takes place of blitzer (OUTSIDE)
Smoke To or Away	Corner	Free safety takes place of blitzer (DEEP)
Blast To or Away	Free Safety	Open

Example Mike Blitz

Example Sam Blitz

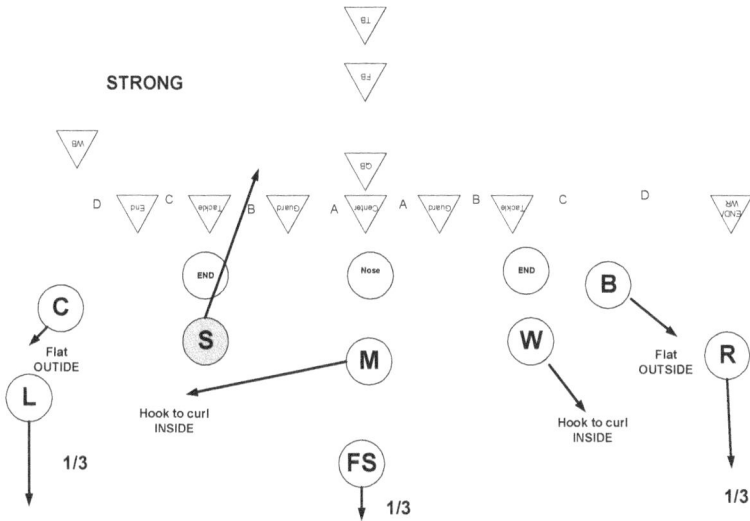

Two player blitz zone Cover 3

When a two linebacker blitz is the called play, this becomes three linebackers under and three defensive backs over coverage. In this coverage, the middle and two outside zones are always covered.

Blitz	Blitzer	Adjustment
Ace and Bang To or Away	Mike – Sam/Will	3 Under – Non-blitzer Sam/Will to middle and Bear and Cub to outside
Ace and Crack To or Away	Mike - Sam/Will	3 Under - – Non-blitzer Sam/Will middle and Bear and Cub to outside
Ace and Lightning To or Away	Mike – Bear/Cub	3 Under – Non-blitzer Sam/Will middle other non-blitzer Sam/Will goes to outside
Bang	Sam and Will	3 Under – Mike stays in

		middle and Bear and Cub stay outside
Crack	Sam and Will	3 Under – Mike stays in middle and Bear and Cub stay to outside
Lightning	Bear and Cub	3 Under – Sam and Will to outside Mike stay in middle
Lightning To or Away and- Crack To or away	Bear/Cub and Sam/Will to same side	3 Under – Mike to outside blitz side Will/Sam not blitzing replace Mike

Example Mike and Sam Blitz

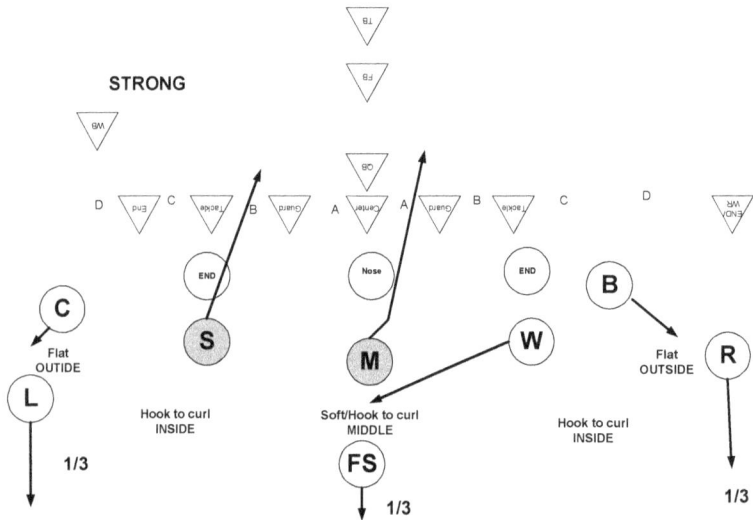

Example Sam and Right Outside Linebacker Blitz

Three man blitz zone Cover 3

With a three man blitz, the coverage is two under and three over. The linebackers make the adjustment to keep the middle open.

Blitz	Blitzer	Adjustment
Ace - Bang	Mike, Sam and Will	OLB cover outside zones
Ace - Crack	Mike, Sam and Will	OLB cover outside zones
Ace - Lighting	Mike, Bear and Cub	Sam and Will cover outside zones

Example Ace – Bang

COACHING POINT: For the youth level, the zone cover 3 concept is the easiest for the players to understand and the coaches to teach. Some years, we never get beyond the cover 3 at the youth level. At the middle school, we start with the cover 3 and we introduce cover 1 as the season progresses. At whatever level, coaches should also ensure players are prepared for adjustments to formations of opponents. Cover 1 or 0 is better for offensive formations that use trips, twins or quads in their formations

NUMERATE PROGRESS

Every player and the team must get better everyday. This is the mantra of every coach. How do you determine if this is true of your team? Many coaches at the youth level have an informal method to evaluate players. Coaches should:

- ➢ Know required skills
- ➢ Know players performance of skills
- ➢ Record and display progress

The following are three examples to numerate progress. They are: player evaluation, player skills development record and depth chart.

Player Evaluation

The player evaluation could be used to assess a player. The coach(es) determine the criteria for the player on a specific team. The criteria are the characteristics determined essential for success on the football team. It should include football and non-football characteristics. The rating scale can be 1-5 or 1-9 with higher number being best. The table below shows an example.

Name	Attitude	Coach ability	Speed	Quick	Overall Rating
Joe	.3.5	4	4.5	4	3.8
Pete	4	4	4	4	4
Ed	3	3	3	3	3
Mike	2	2	2	2	2
Jim	1	1	1	1	1
Ty	2.5	2.5	2.5	2.5	2.5
Devyn	5	5	5	5	5

Player Skills Development Report

The player skills development report shows the required skills for a specific position along with the date of skill training, an evaluation of success, and finally date the player became proficient in the skill. The column for "needs improvement" could state the specific action the player needs to work on to become proficient.

Inside Linebacker

Skill	Train Date	Needs Improvement	Proficient
Stance			
Movement			
Stun			
Stun & Shed			
Head on Tackling			
Angle Tackling			
Open Field Tackling			
Side Line Tackling			
Pursuit Run			
Pursuit Pass			
Ball Strip			
Ball Strip Punch			
Ball Strip Pull			
Fumble Recovery			
Scoop and Score			
Pass Coverage Zone			
Pass Coverage Man			

The overall display of progress for a football team is the depth chart. As a minimum, this is the progress report. Every team needs a depth chart. This depth chart should be displayed or shown to the players. It should be updated as necessary, but the players should know their position before each game. Figure 12 shows defense depth chart.

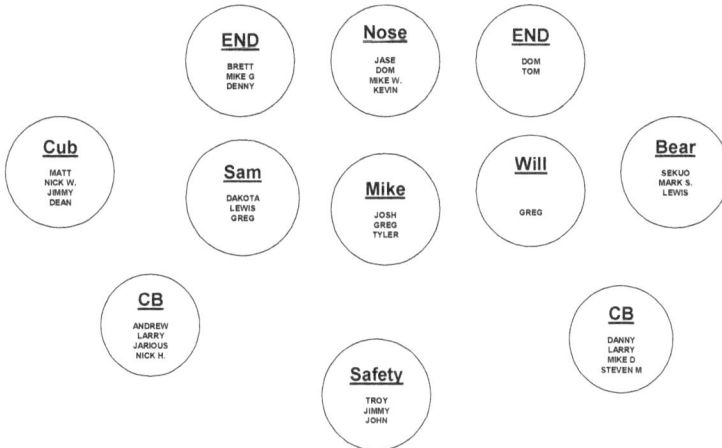

Figure 12. Defense Depth Chart.

3-5-3 Defense

CHAPTER 6
ALLOW FUN

ALLOW FUN

It is essential at the youth and middle school level to make it fun. The following is outline to make it fun.

Foster a defense mindset

Use a playbook for the defense

Nurture perfect practice

FOSTER DEFENSE MINDSET

As stated many times throughout this book, the 3-5-3 defense is an aggressive and attacking defense that must have discipline to maintain responsibilities. This is challenging at the youth and middle school levels. This requires a special mindset in every defensive player. The coach needs to foster this mindset. First, the coach develops players that can perform the specific responsibilities of the defense. They must be able to make plays. Also, they must buy into the idea of a penetrating, pursuing and punishing defense. This requires them to act with enthusiasm. In addition, the coach ensures players show progress everyday. The coach sparks in every defensive player the desire to be part of every play. In addition, they must know the importance of team defense. Finally, the coach promotes a defensive players mindset that includes an obsession with his/her best and the need for success.

Perform - penetrate, pursue and punish (hit hard)

Act with enthusiasm

Show progress everyday

Spark desire to be part of every play

Involve "team"

Obsess for excellence (doing his/her best)

Need for success

USE DEFENSE PLAYBOOK

The defensive playbook is a major component of success with the 3-5-3 defense. At the youth level, the defensive players enjoy that they have a playbook just like the offense.

Defensive Huddle

The defense can use a huddle to call the specific play. The following describes the defensive huddle alignment.

1. Line Up
    A. Front row (L-E-N-E-R)
        1. Feet shoulder width apart and parallel
        2. Toe to toe and side-by side
        3. Hands on knees with head up looking at Mike backer
    B. Back row (C-S-FS-W-B)
        1. Feet shoulder width apart and parallel
        2. Toe to toe and side to side
        3. Standing
        4. Head up looking at Mike backer

---

2. Calling the Defense
 A. Nose holds up hand and calls the huddle 3 yards form the ball
 B. Safety calls the down and distance
 C. Mike calls the defense
 D. Mike yells "Ready"
 E. Everyone claps hands and yells "TEAM NAME"
 F. Everyone hustles to position
 G. When the center's hand goes down on the ball we should be ready to play
 H. **ABSOLUTELY NO TALKING IN THE HUDDLE**
 I. Mike calls the strong "run" side
 J. Free safety calls the strong "pass" side

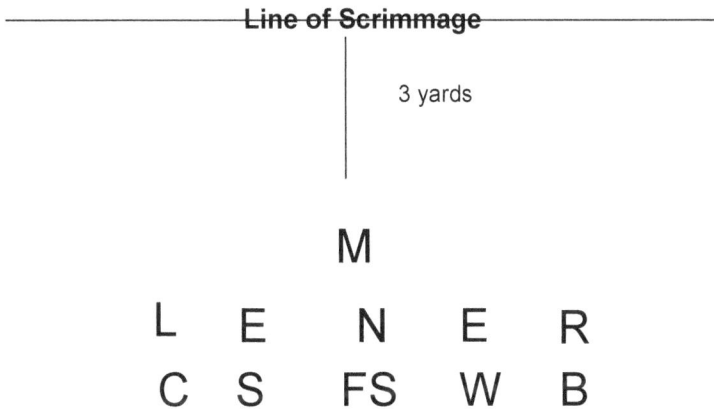

Line of Scrimmage

3 yards

M

L E N E R
C S FS W B

Figure 13. Basic Huddle for 3-5-3

COACHING POINT: You can option not have any huddle. If you do not use a huddle, you can have the players communicate the defensive assignment to each other or you can use wrist coaches for each player.

Defense Plays

The following is a sample wristband for 30 plays. The following pages shows the plays call diagrams.

	DL	Blitz	Cover	
0	Stack	None	3	M
1	Stack Weak	Ace **To**	3	M
2	Stack Strong	Ace Away	3	M
3	Pinch Strong	Ace Away	3	M
4	Slant Weak	Ace **To**	3	M
5	Stack Strong	Bang **To**	3	S
6	Angle Weak	Bang Away	3	W
7	Pinch Strong	Crack **To**	3	S
8	Angle Strong	Crack **To**	3	S
9	Slant Strong	Crack Away	3	W
10	Pinch Strong	Lightning **To**	3	OS
11	Slant Strong	Lightning Away	3	OW
12	Slant Strong	Blast **To**	3	FS
13	Stack Strong	Bang	3	S – W
14	Pinch Strong	Crack	3	S – W
15	Stack Strong	Ace Away - Lightning **To**	3	M – OS
16	Stack Weak	Ace **To** - Bang **To**	3	M – S
17	Stack Weak	Ace To - Bang Away	3	M – W
18	Pinch Weak	Ace To - Crack **To**	3	M – S
19	Pinch Strong	Lightning	3	OS – OW
20	Slant Strong	Bang **To** - Lightning **To**	3	S – OS
21	Angle Weak	Bang Away - Lightning Away	3	W – OW
22	Angle Strong	Crack **To** - Lightning **To**	3	S – OS
23	Pinch Strong	Crack **To** - Lightning Away	3	S – OW
24	Stack Weak	Ace **To** - Blast	1	M - FS
25	Angle Weak	Ace **To** - Crack **To** - Bang Away	3	M – S-W
26	Slant Weak	Ace **To** - Lighting Away	3	M – OW
27	Slant Strong	Lightning Away - Smoke Away	3	OW – CB
28	Stack Strong	Lightning **To** - Blast **To**	3	OS – FS
29	Stack Weak	Ace **To** - Bang - Lighting	3	M–S-W-OS-OW
30	Stack Strong	Ace Away - Bang	3	M-S-W

COACHING POINT: Some coaches elect to just call plays without a set playbook. They do not like to limit plays to a certain number. The potential number of plays using the 3-5-3 defense using all combination can be over 100 plays. These coaches use hand signals to communicate the many plays. In order to keep it simple, we have been successful with 26 - 30 plays. These are the number of readable plays that fit on a youth (26) or regular (30) wristband.

STACK NONE – COVER 3

STRONG

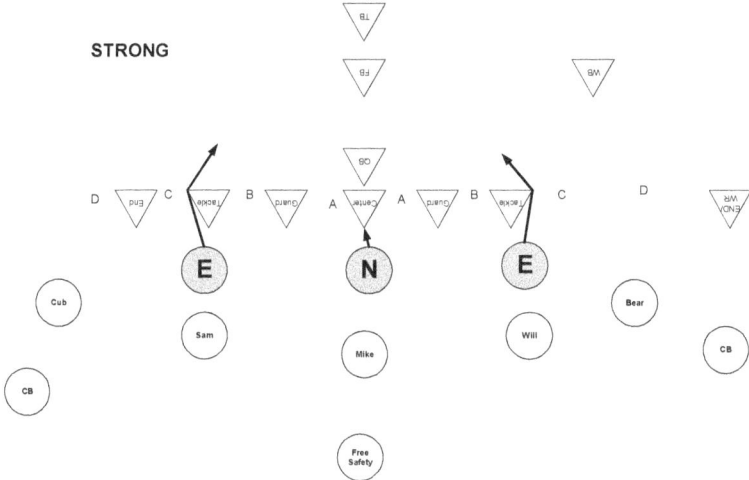

STACK WEAK - ACE TO - COVER 3

STRONG

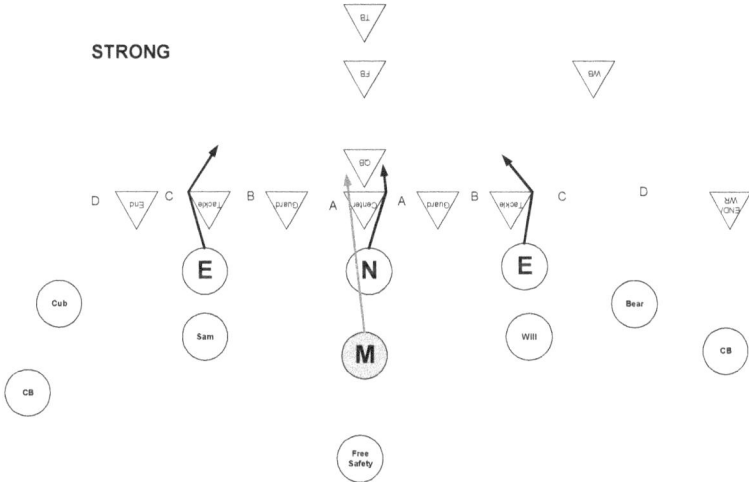

STACK STRONG – ACE AWAY – COVER 3

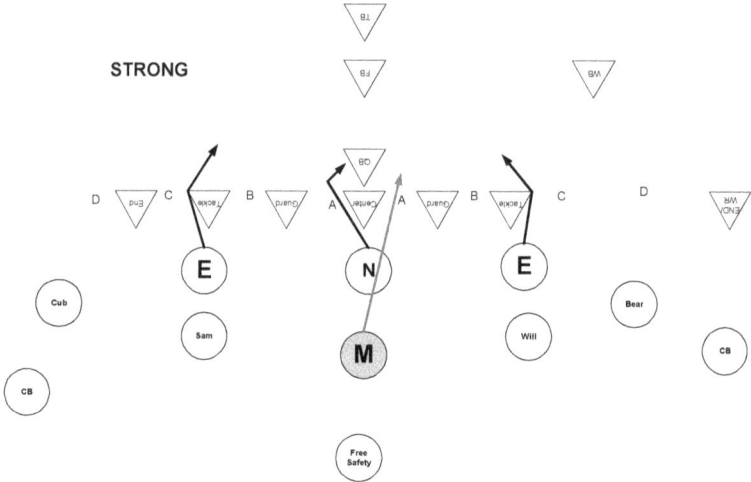

PINCH STRONG – ACE AWAY – COVER 3

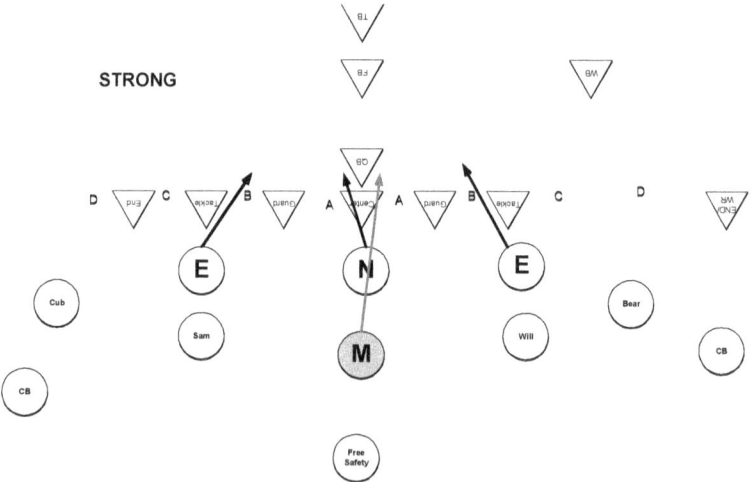

SLANT WEAK – ACE TO – COVER 3

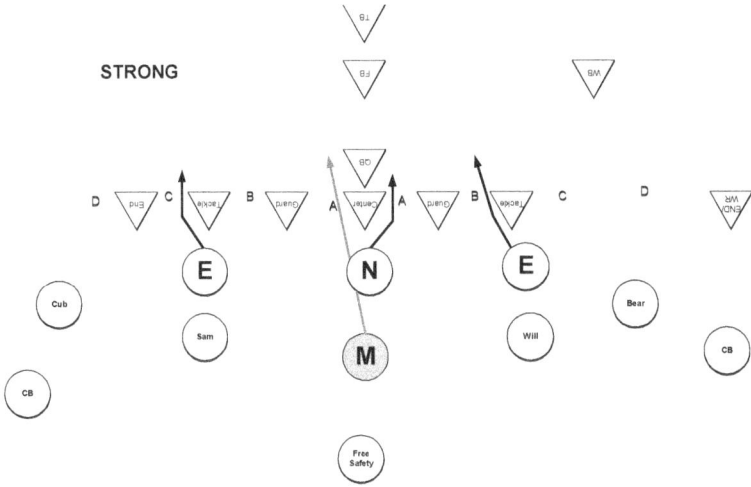

STACK STRONG - BANG TO - COVER 3

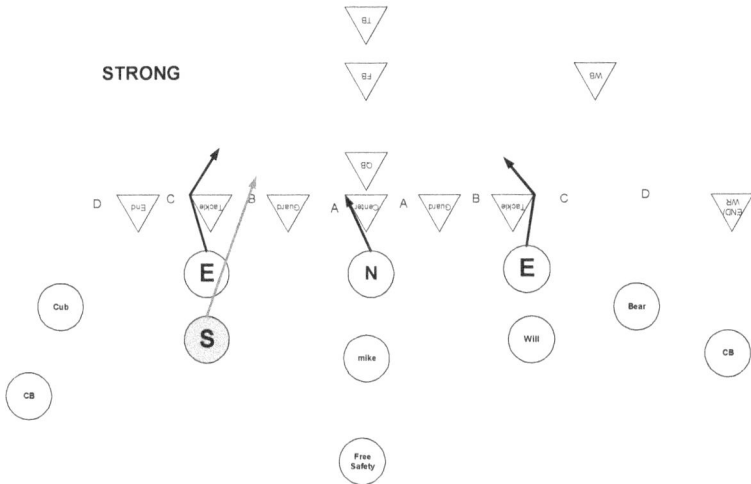

3-5-3 Defense

ANGLE WEAK - BANG AWAY – COVER 3

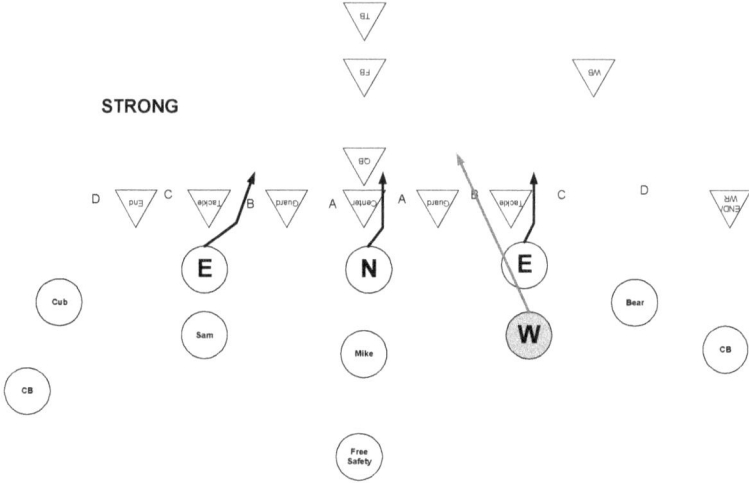

PINCH STRONG - CRACK TO – COVER 3

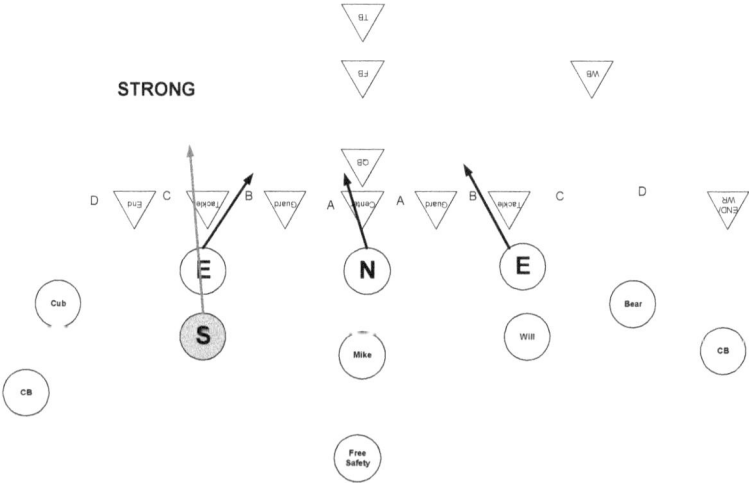

ANGLE STRONG - CRACK TO – COVER 3

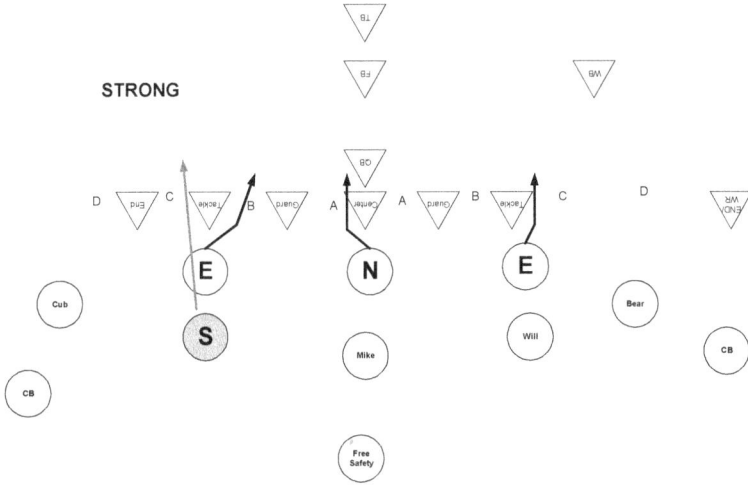

STRONG

SLANT STRONG - CRACK AWAY – COVER 3

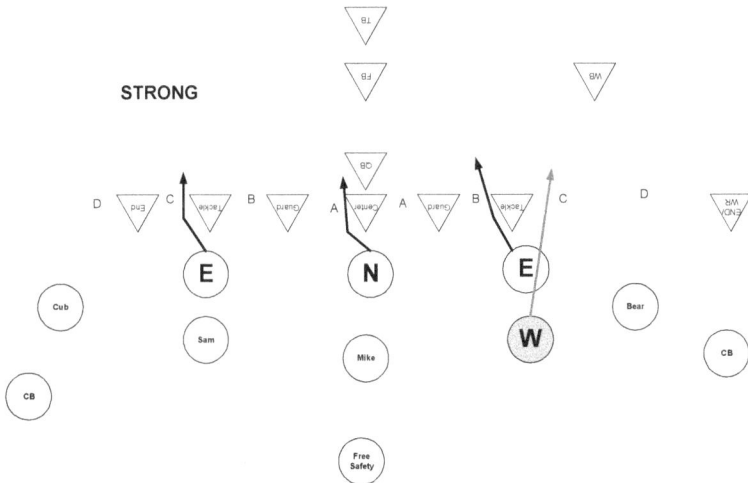

STRONG

PINCH STRONG - LIGHTNING TO – COVER 3

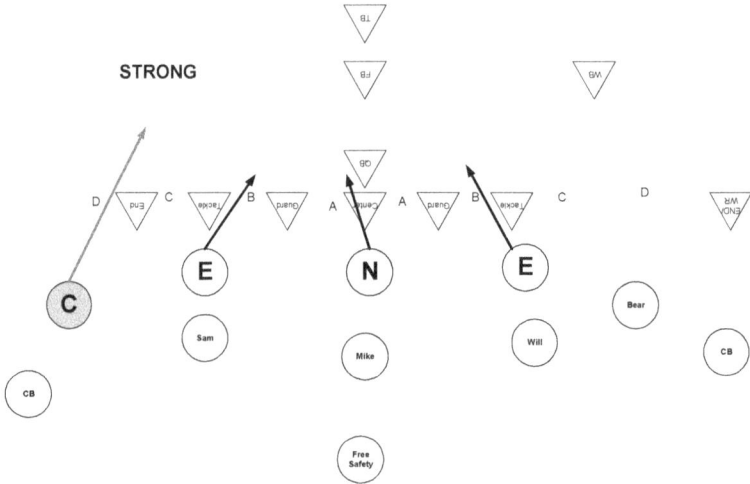

SLANT STRONG - LIGHTNING AWAY – COVER 3

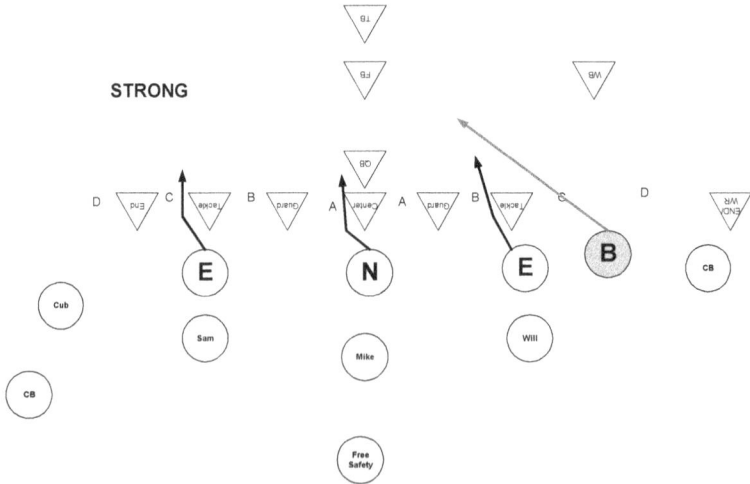

SLANT STRONG - BLAST TO – COVER 3

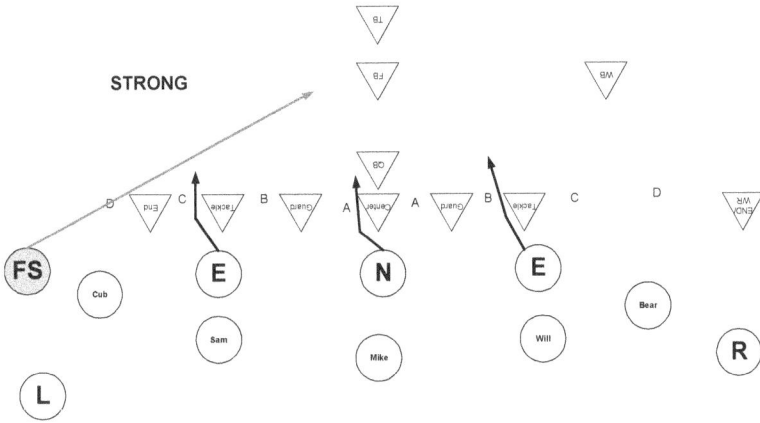

STACK STRONG – BANG – COVER 3

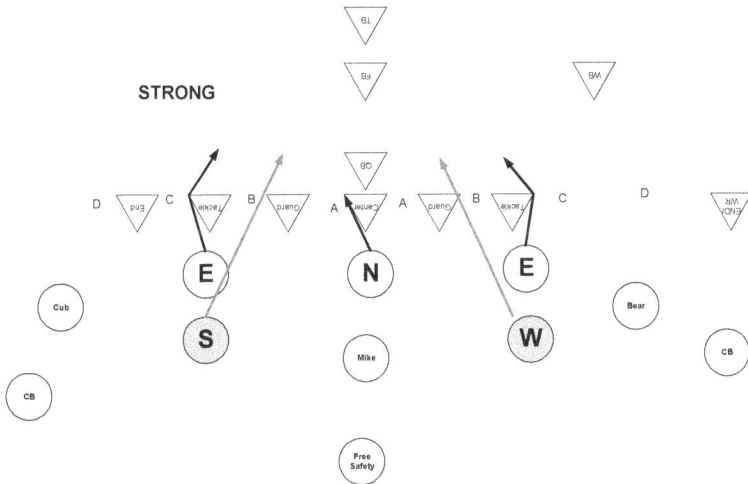

PINCH STRONG – CRACK – COVER 3

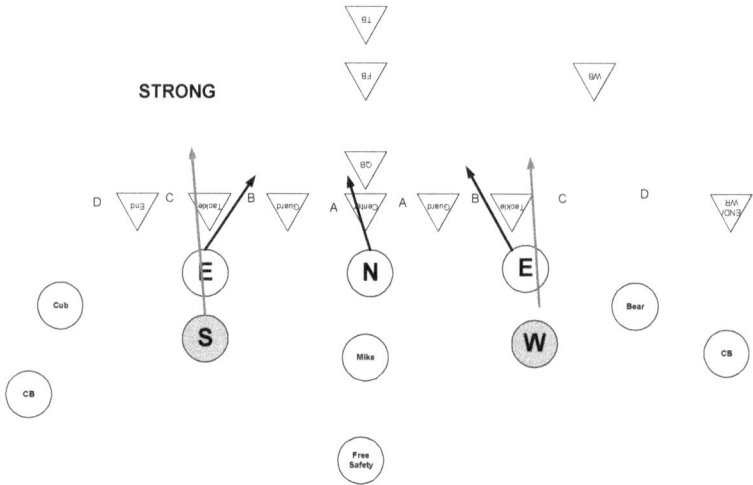

STACK STRONG - ACE AWAY - LIGHTNING TO – COVER 3

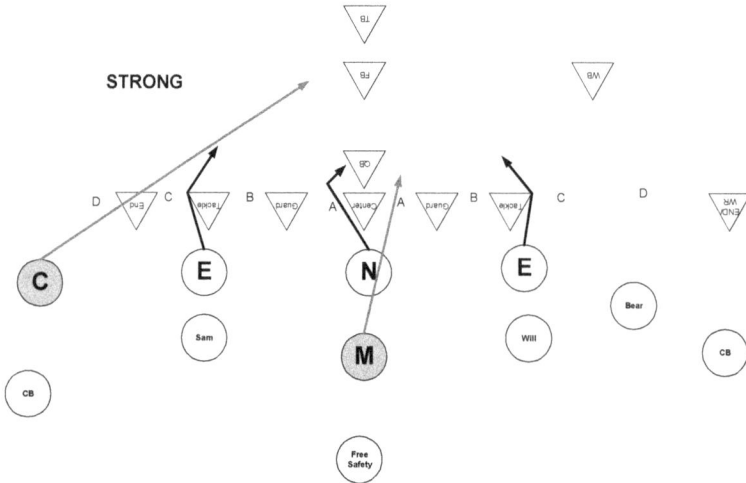

STACK WEAK - ACE TO - BANG TO – COVER 3

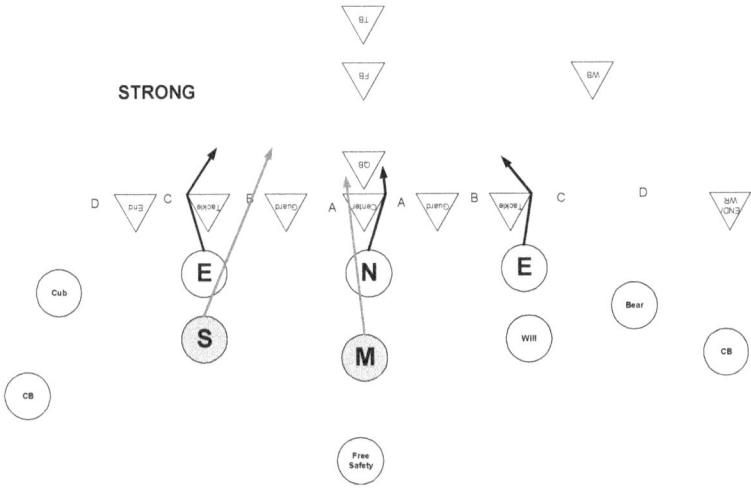

STACK WEAK - ACE TO - BANG AWAY – COVER 3

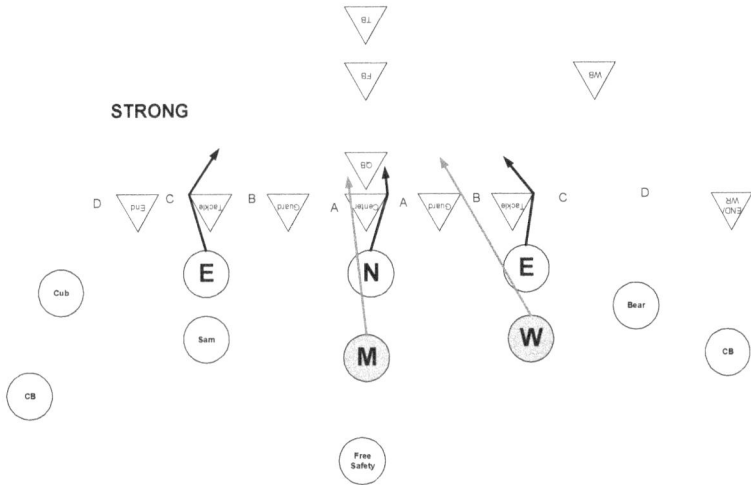

PINCH WEAK - ACE TO - CRACK TO – COVER 3

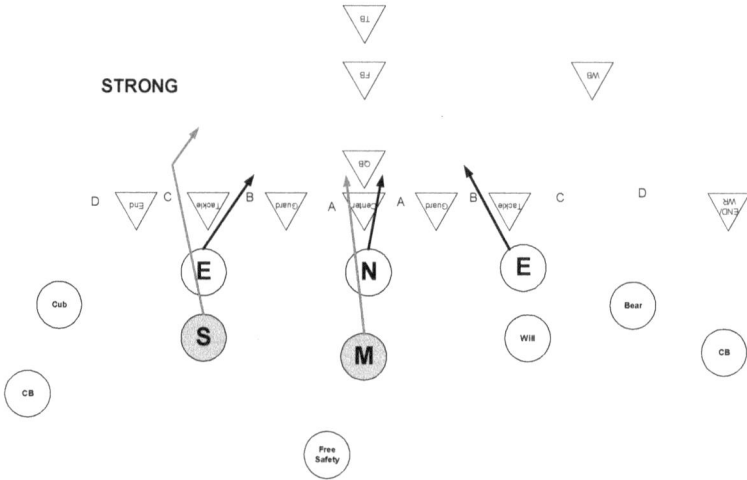

PINCH STRONG – LIGHTNING – COVER 3

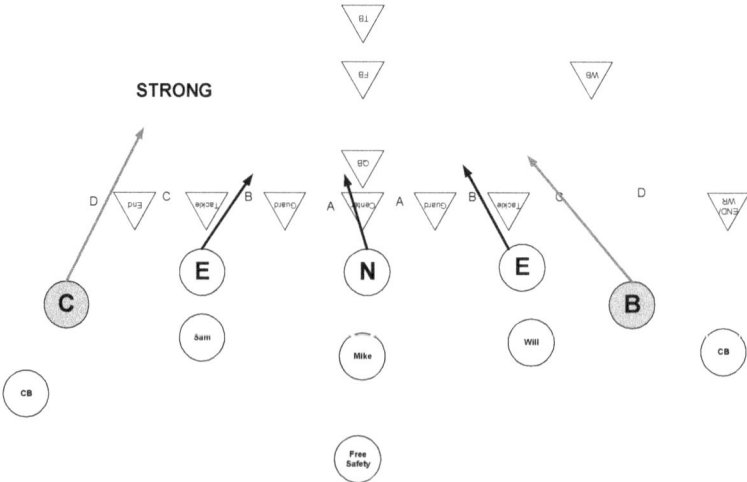

SLANT STRONG - BANG TO - LIGHTNING TO – COVER 3

ANGLE WEAK - BANG AWAY- LIGHTNING AWAY – COVER 3

ANGLE STRONG - CRACK TO - LIGHTNING TO – COVER 3

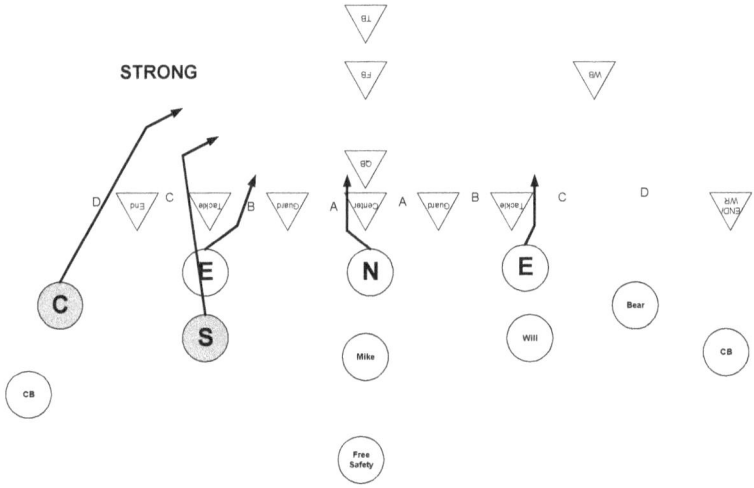

PINCH STRONG - CRACK TO - LIGHTNING AWAY – COVER 3

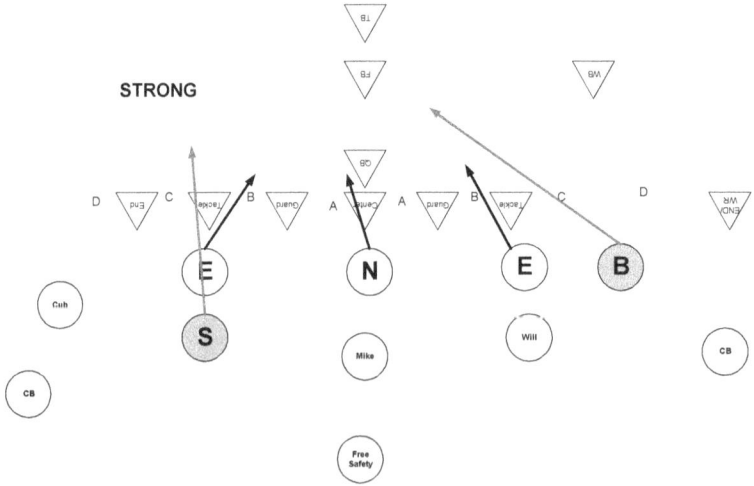

STACK WEAK - ACE TO – BLAST – COVER 3

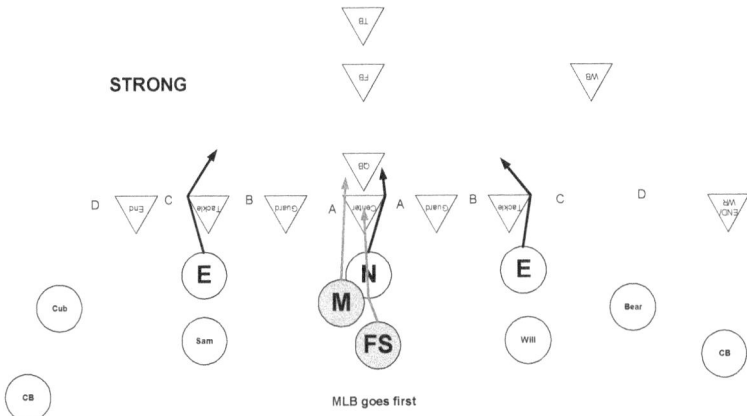

MLB goes first

ANGLE WEAK - ACE TO - CRACK TO - BANG AWAY – COVER 3

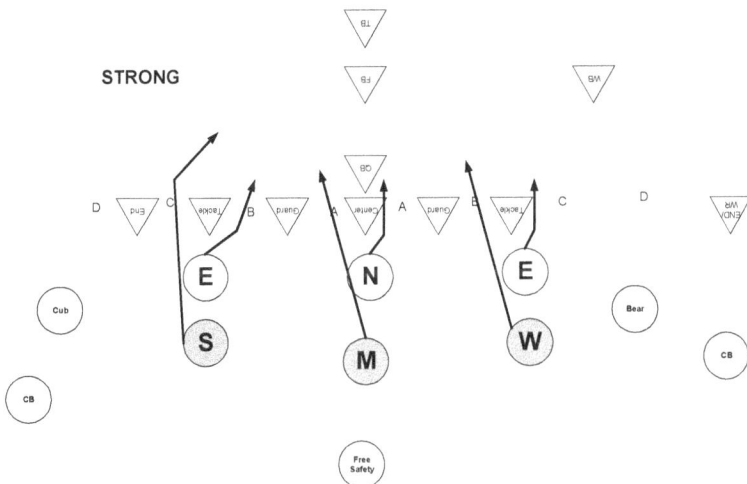

SLANT WEAK - ACE TO - LIGHTING AWAY – COVER 3

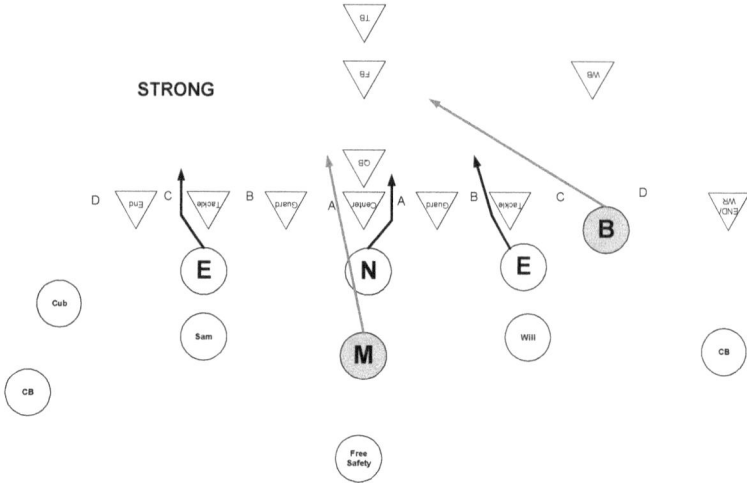

SLANT STRONG - LIGHTNING AWAY - SMOKE AWAY – COVER 3

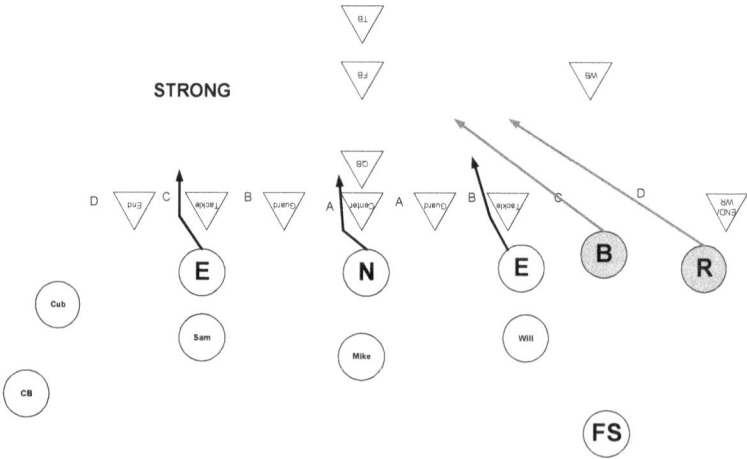

STACK STRONG - LIGHTNING TO - BLAST TO – COVER 3

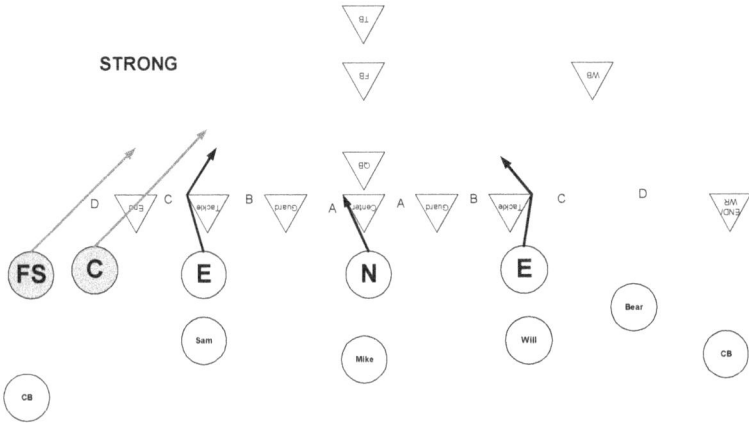

STACK WEAK - ACE TO – BANG – LIGHTING – COVER 3

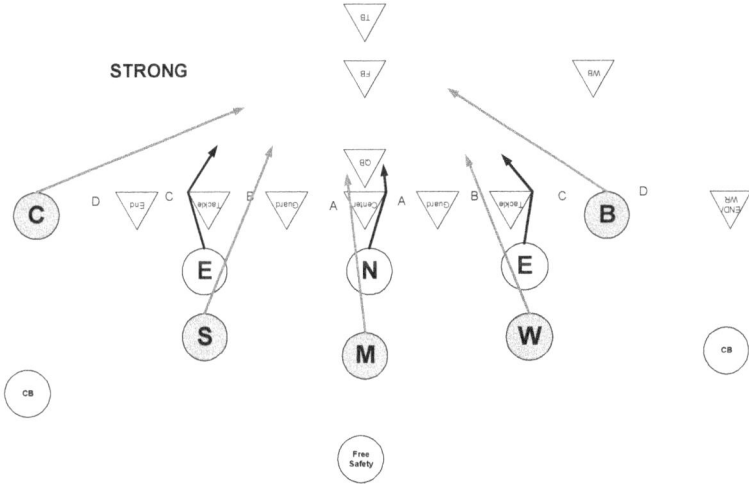

STACK STRONG - ACE AWAY- BANG - COVER 3

NURTURE PERFECT PRACTICE

The time for practice is precious. Coaches must make the most of the time on the practice field.

COACHING POINT: Every practice must have an overall objective and every drill must support accomplishing the overall objective. Coaches should not just drill for drill sake without using a drill to make a specific improvement in the player(s) or the team.

Practice Plan

Perfect practice starts with a perfect plan. Planning is the difference in failure or success of any program. At the youth level, planning is sometimes adhoc or missing altogether. This is where a team can gain an advantage that not only benefits the team, but proper planning is an advantage to each player's development. Ideally, a coach will have a season long plan. This is not always possible or practical at the youth levels. However, a weekly practice plan and a daily practice plan can be reasonable to provide the basic plans for perfect practice.

Weekly Practice Plan

The weekly practice plans provide an outline for the week's practices. It is the foundation for the daily practice plan.

The table below shows an example of a weekly practice plan.

PRACTICE WEEK 1 - DEFENSE

DAY	Monday	Wednesday	Thursday	Friday
FOCUS	RUN DEFENSE	RUN DEFENSE	PASS DEFENSE	DEFENSE
INDIVIDUALS				
D-LINE	Line Stance Step Step and Rip Nose 　Strong/Weak DE 　Stack – Pinch	Stance Step Step and Rip Nose 　Strong/Weak DE 　Stack – Pinch 　Slant- Angle	Stance Step Step and Rip Nose 　Strong/Weak DE 　Stack – Pinch 　Slant- Angle	REVIEW
LINEBACKERS	Linebackers Stances Movement Basic Stun Blitzes 　Ace 　Bang 　Crack 　Lighting	Linebackers Stances Basic Stun Tackling - Form Pursuit	Linebackers Stances Movement Stun Tackling – Mat Straight - Angle Multi Man Blitz Pass Drops Scope and Score	REVIEW
DEFENSE BACK	Stance Movement Cover 　Cover 3	Stance Movement Blitzes: 　: Smoke 　Blast	Stance Movement Covers	REVIEW

　　　　　　　3-5-3 Defense

Daily Practice Plan

The daily practice plan must have a practice objective. In addition, it should outline the basic format for the practice. In the example daily practice plan, the outline for the practice includes: dynamic warm-up, individual sessions and a team session. Finally, the daily practice plan shows the skills and the specific drills to develop the skills.

An example of a daily practice plan follows.

PRACTICE PLAN
WEEK 1 – DAY 1

EQUIPMENT: HELMETS ONLY
OBJECTIVES: Provide fundamental DEFENSE skills training.

TIME		ACTIVITY	COMMENTS/DRILLS
20 MIN	TEAM	DYNAMIC WARM-UP	
10 MIN	POSITION INDIVIDUAL	AGILITY AND SPEED	
30 – 45 MIN	POSITION INDIVIDUAL	SKILLS AND DRILLS	
30 – 45 MIN	TEAM	TEAM	
15 MIN	TEAM	CONDITIONING	

	SKILLS	DRILLS
OBJECTIVES	FUNDAMENTALS Stance Movement Position Basics DL LB DB Basic Defense	
D-LINE	Gap responsibilities Stance First Step Movement Basics (step and rip)	Birddog

LB	Gap Responsibilities Stance Movement	Birddog
DB	Responsibilities Stance Movement	Birddog

TEAM	TEAM
	Basic defense overview
	   Formation (Basic)
	   Alignment and Gaps
		Team drill

ALLOW TIME FOR WATER BREAKS

COACHING POINT: A telltale sign that a coach does not have a specific plan to improve defensive skills is when the players are doing nothing but the NO items listed on the tackling general instructions.

Drill for Skills

At defensive practice, there is some drills that are repeated every time and there are some drills that are performed from time-to-time. The skills that must be worked on every single defensive practice include the following:

> Position agilities
> Stance
> Movement
> Pursuit
> Defeat the block
> Tackling – Position dominate
> Individual Position Play
> Team Plays

The skills that need to be practiced not every day include some of the following:

- Strip the ball (All)
- Fall on ball (All)
- Scoop and score (LB)
- Pass Interception (LB)
- Defeat the Block other than stun (LB)
- Tackling – non position dominate

COACHING POINT: If the coach does not have a standard drill to make a specific improvement required for the player(s) or the team. The simplest method is to design a drill that duplicates the actual skill's use in a game-like situation.

Specific Drills

The following are specific drills for general skills and position particular skills.

- Defensive line drill three point stance
- Getting off the ball
- First step defensive line
- Step and rip down the line by defensive line
- Defensive line plays
- Stance run and football position
- Deliver a blow
- Pursuit defensive line
- Pass rush defensive line
- Stun progression
- Stun and throw
- Stun deliver a blow

- Attack the blocker
- Defeat the block outside linebacker
- Defeat the block all linebackers
- Form tackling
- Tackling three whistle drill
- Tackling on the mat
- Tackling - head-on
- Tackling - angle
- Tackling - increase the distance
- Tackling - the blocker and tackle
- Tackling to the hole
- Tackling - open field
- Tackling - sideline
- Tackling - gang
- Tackling – goal line
- Pursuit lane drill linebackers
- Strip ball
- Fumble recovery
- Defense Back – stance and backpedal
- Defense Back – turn and run
- Defensive Back - direction
- Defense Back – backpedal angle
- Defense Back – backpedal tag
- Pass coverage – zone drops
- Team defensive plays

Defensive Line Drill Three Point Stance

The coach has the defensive line (DL) spread out in one or more lines facing him (birddog). On command from the coach, the defensive line assumes the proper defensive stance.

- Stand straight up with feet together
- Move feet out even to the hip width or slightly wider
- Keep toes pointed straight ahead
- Bend knees so forearms rest on inside of thighs
- Reach straight out with hand right or left hand (right or left handed)
- Place hand on ground slightly (three fingers) ahead of shoulder pads
- Keep shoulders even with back straight
- Have weight on hand and balls of feet
- Keep head up and eyes straight ahead

Drill Coaching Point: Maintain proper stance

DL   DL   DL   DL

DL   DL   DL   DL

Coach

NOTE: This same drill can be used for any stance.

Drill Getting Off the Ball

The coach has the defensive line (DL) line up on a line. The coach kneels down with one hand on the ball place in front of him. Defensive lineman get in stance, each makes sure they can see the ball. As the coach moves the ball, the linemen should charge straight ahead sprinting five yards. ADVANCE: Defensive lineman makes step and rip and sprint.

Drill Coaching Point: Defensive linemen react to movement of the ball as the center snaps the ball.

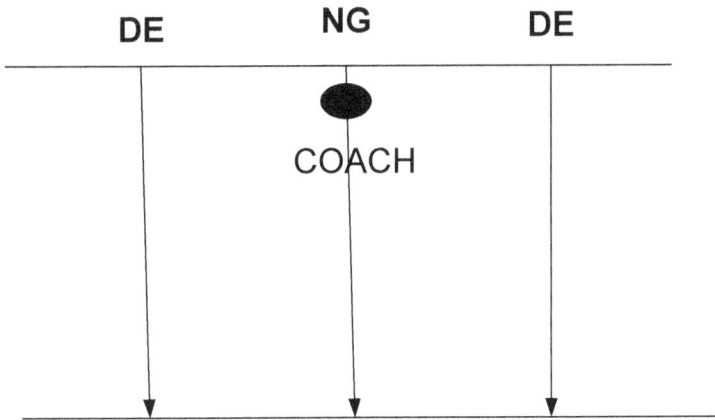

NOTE: It is a good idea to use a football on a stick (hockey stick) to simulate center snaps.

First Step Drill Defensive Line

The coach has the defensive line spread out in one or more lines facing him. On command from the coach, the defensive linemen assume the proper defensive stance. On command from the coach, the defensive linemen take first step (right then left).

Progression: The defensive lineman step and rip.

Drill Coaching Point: Get to the gap and make forward progress.

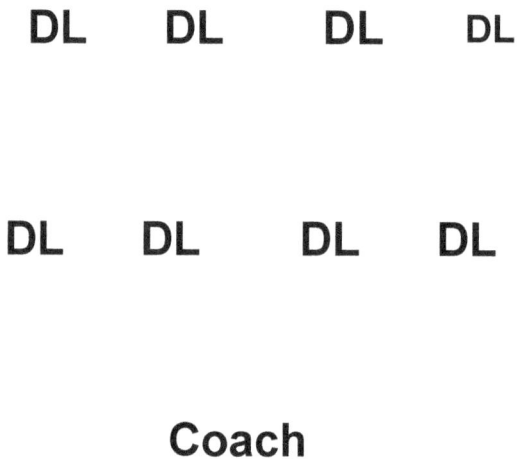

DL   DL   DL   DL

DL   DL   DL   DL

Coach

Step and Rip Down the Line by Defensive Line

The coach has the defensive line (DL) line-up on yard line or sideline. On command from the coach, the defensive linemen assume the proper defensive stance. On command from the coach, the defensive lineman take first step right and then left down the line.

Progression: The defensive lineman step and rip down the line first right and then left.

Drill Coaching Point: Step across the line and make progress down the line.

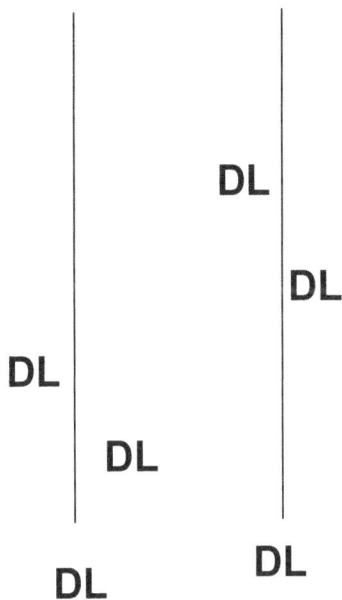

Defensive Line Plays

The coach has the defensive line assume defensive positions. The coach calls the defensive line play. The defensive linemen assume the proper defensive stance. On command from the coach, the defensive line executes the play.

Play Calls:

> - Stack
> - Stack Weak
> - Stack Strong
> - Pinch Strong
> - Pinch Weak
> - Slant Weak
> - Slant Strong
> - Angle Weak
> - Angle Strong

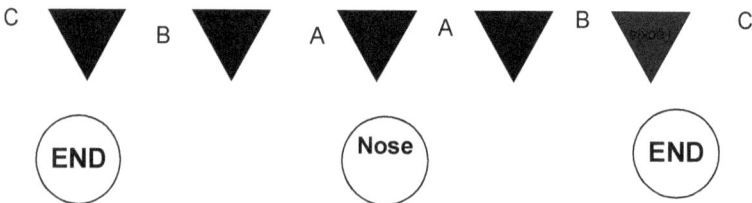

Stance Run and Football Position

The coach has the defensive players spread out in one or more lines facing him. On command from the coach, the defensive players (LB) assume the proper defensive stance. On command from the coach, the defensive players sprint at full speed to the coach, gather, and get into a good hitting (football) position.

LB   **LB**   **LB**   **LB**

LB   **LB**   **LB**   **LB**

Coach

Deliver a Blow

Defensive player (DL) and blocker (B) kneel facing each other about 12 inches apart. Defensive player leans back on heels. The blocker gives a forward lean. On command, the defensive player launches forward and delivers a blow to the chest of blocker. The defensive player follows through as much as possible.

Progression: Do the same from a standing position.

Drill Coaching Point:: Defensive player must not overextend arms while delivering the blow. See how far defensive player can move the blocker back.

B　　**B**　　**B**

DL　　**DL**　　**DL**

Coach

NOTE: Team can use the same drill for tackling. Instead of delivering a blow, the tackler rotates hips, eyes to the sky and wraps.

Pursuit Defensive Line

Defensive lineman takes position in front of bag/offensive lineman. The coach calls the stunt. The coach tells the running back (RB) to run right or left. On command, the defensive lineman (DL) does the stunt and the RB goes the direction. Defensive lineman gets to the gap finds the ball and goes to the RB to make the tackle. Coach makes calls to the gap and away from the gap to practice change of direction.

Drill Coaching Point: Make sure the defensive lineman does the stunt properly with step and rip technique.

RB

DL

COACH

NOTE: Coaches can use the same drill for linebackers. The coach calls the blitz. The linebacker blitzes the gap and then pursues the running back.

Pass Rush Defensive Line

All three defensive linemen take proper position in front of a bag or an offensive lineman. The coach calls the stunt. The coach tells the quarterback (QB) take pass drop. On command, the defensive lineman does the stunt and the QB goes the specific drop. Defensive linemen gets to the gap finds the QB and makes pass rush.

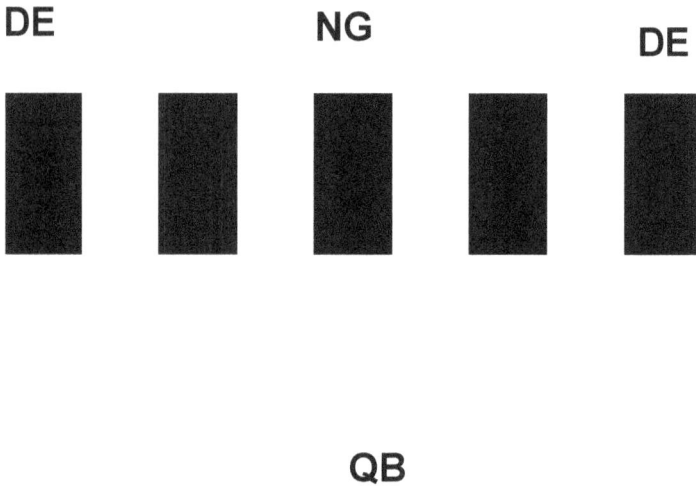

DE   **NG**   **DE**

QB

NOTE: This drill can be done along with linebackers or the linebackers can do the same drill without the lineman.

Stun Progression

1. KNEEL Linebacker (LB) and blocker (B) knell facing each other about 12 inches apart. LB leans back on heels. The blocker gives a forward lean. On command, the LB launches forward and delivers a blow to the chest of B. LB follows through as much as possible.
2. STAND From the standing position, LB positions his hands with head straight in. On command, the LB grabs and pushes the B back keeping hold.
3. THROW Same as above on the LB throws the B to left or right.

Drill Coaching Point: LB must not overextend arms while delivering the blow. See how far linebacker can move the blocker. Check hand position.

B   B   B

LB   LB   LB

Coach

Stun and Throw

Linebacker (LB) and blocker (B) stand facing each other about 12 inches apart. LB positions hands on blocker in proper stun position. Blocker gives a forward lean. On command, the LB stuns the Blocker, grabs and throws the blocker to the side (right and left).

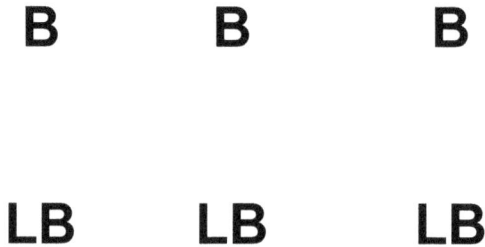

B   **B**   **B**

LB   **LB**   **LB**

Coach

Stun Deliver a Blow

1.	Linebacker (LB) takes a ready position about 2 feet from a blocker (B). The linebacker delivers a blow to the blocker using the same shoulder and foot forward.

2.	LB takes a ready position about 2 feet from two blockers. The blockers are about 12 to 18 inches apart. The blocker on the right steps toward the LB. The LB delivers a blow to the blocker using the same shoulder and foot forward. Steps back and then steps toward the other blocker with the proper shoulder and finally steps back. REPEAT several times.

Progression: Use on LB and one B. Have the B move to the right or left and have the LB react and place hands in proper position with proper foot forward.

Drill 1

B

Coach

LB

Drill 2

B   **B**

Coach

LB

Attack the Blocker

Drill 1: The coach has the one linebacker (LB) and one blocker (B) on opposite side of a bag. The blocker holds a impact shield. On command from the coach, the LB assumes the proper defensive football stance. On command from the coach, the LB attacks the blocker, stuns and drives player backwards.
Drill 2: Coach can use defensive lineman and linebacker and two blockers or use complete left or right half of line or use complete offensive line.

Progression: Do scoop and score or tackle at end.

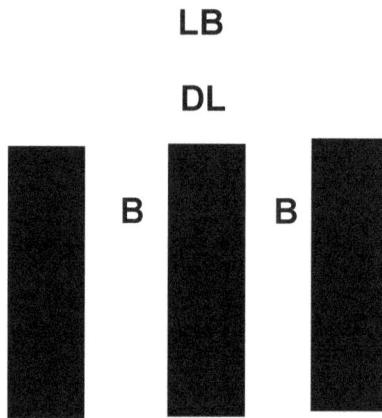

LB

DL

B   B

Defeat the Block Outside Linebacker

Align three offensive players in power I or I formation. One offensive player is on the line to represent a tight end (TE). The other two offensive players are in the backfield in the "I" or power "I" formation. Position the outside linebacker (OLB) in normal alignment to the TE. On command from the coach or center snap, the blockers try to block OLB. In turn the OLB try to get pass the TE and takes on and defeats the two blocks of the backfield while maintaining outside leverage

Progression: Coach can make the third offensive player be a ball-carrier. Have the defensive player tackle (wrap and drive). Coach can have the third offensive player be a bag. The coach can have the defensive player tackle the bag or do a fumble recovery.

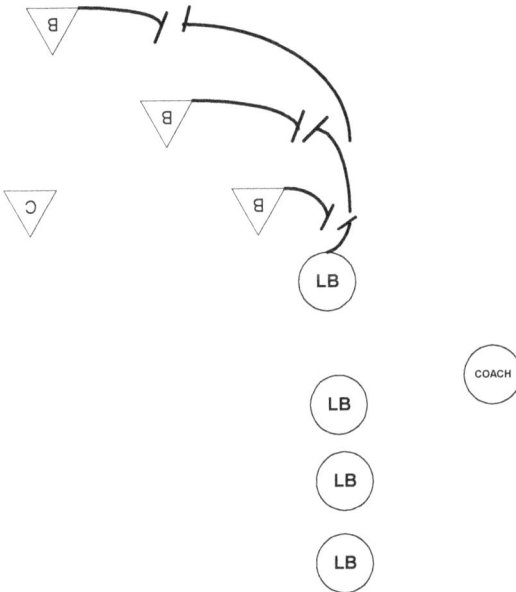

Defeat the Blocker All Linebackers

Align linebackers (LB) in normal position. Position blockers (B) and running back (RB) at various position to allow the LB to defeat a block and get in position to make the tackle.

Progression: Use blocker(s) and RB and have LB pursue, attack the blocker(s) and make the tackle.

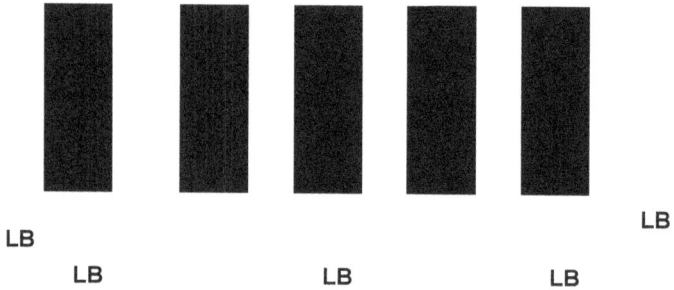

Form Tackling

FIT: The coach has the defensive player (DP) and runner (RB) face each other 6 inches apart. DP is fitted to RB in proper contact position. DP knees bent and hips lowered and back straight and head up. His eyes focused on numbers (chest) of RB.

FIT AND LIFT: On command the designated defenders walk up to their partner and into a good fit position. On the next command they follow through, rolling their hips and lifting their partner and taking him back a few steps.

FORM TACKLING: Partners should be about 5 yards apart. On command the designated offender jogs toward the defender. The defender meets him in proper tackling position and performs a form tackle. Have OP jog in a 45° angle also. Use left and right shoulder.

Drill Coaching Point: Maintain proper technique at all times. Keep head up and rotate hips and drive through ball carrier. Develop form, explosion and strength.

RB

DP

Coach

Tackling Three Whistle Drill

The defensive player (DP) and runner (RB) face each other 12 inches apart. The defensive player execute the steps of a form tackle on whistle commands of the coach.

WHISTLE DRILL:
> Whistle one: step into **HIT** position.
> Whistle two **WRAP**.
> Whistle three lift and **DRIVE**

Drill Coaching Point: Have players call out "HIT," "WRAP," and "DRIVE." Ensure proper technique.

RB

DP

Coach

Tackling on Mat

The coach place a mat on the ground. The ball carrier holds the impact shield for protection. At a coach's signal, the tackler attacks the ball carrier with a form tackle, lifting the ball carrier onto the landing surface. The mat tackling is done straight on, and angle right and left.

Drill Coaching Point: Form tackle, good lift, drive hard. Keep players moving at high speed, and try for a maximum number of reps per player. If a player has a problem with a certain area, such as forgetting to keep his head up, remind him with positive reinforcement before his next rep.

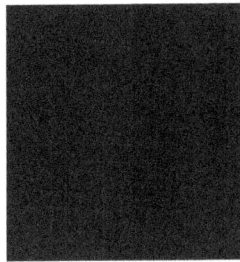

DP

DP

NOTE: At the youth and middle school level, mat tackling is great to start tackling in the preseason to develop proper technique and instill confidence in young players. If you cannot find a mat, line up bags side-by-side to form a flat surface.

Tackling – Head-On

The coach has the two defensive players (DP) on opposite side of a bag. One DP represents the RB. He or she holds an impact shield. On command from the coach, the other DP or tackler (T) assumes the proper defensive football stance. On command the coach, the tackler runs and form tackles the RB and drives player backwards for five yards.

Progression: Coach can have the RB move forward on the bag to ensure the tacklers keep feet apart.

Drill Coaching Point: Maintain proper position for the hit, Keep feet apart along the dummy and at point of impact. Rotate hips and drive.

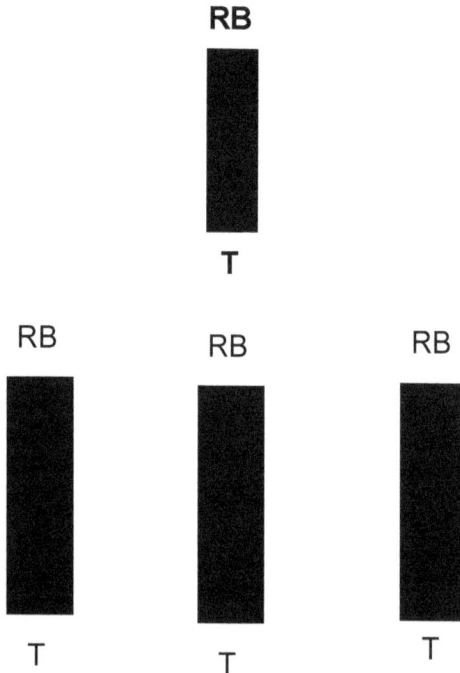

RB

■

T

RB   **RB**   **RB**

■   ■   ■

T   T   T

Tackling - Angle

The coach has the two defensive players (DP) on opposite side of a bag. One DP represents the RB holds a impact shield. On command from the coach, the other DP, the tackler (T), assumes the proper defensive football stance. On command from the coach, the tackler runs and form tackles the other player and drives player backwards from 5 yards.

Drill Coaching Point: Maintain proper position for the hit, keep feet apart along the dummy and at point of impact. Rotate hips and drive.

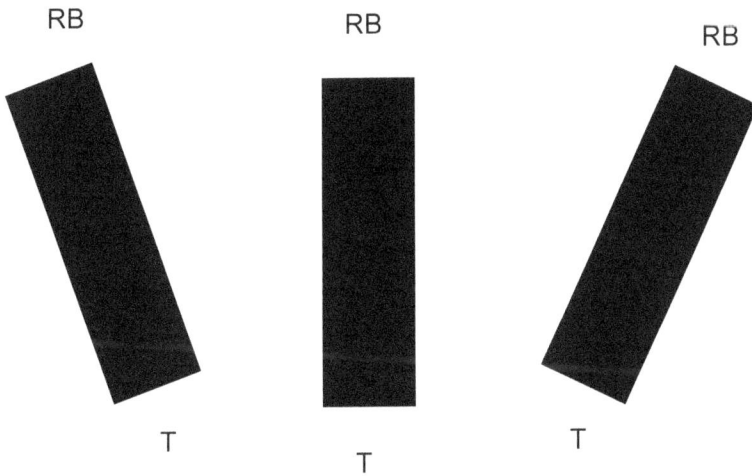

RB RB RB

T T T

Tackling – Increase the Distance

The coach has the two defensive players (DP) on opposite side of a bag. In this drill, the bag is placed five yards from the tackler. One DP represents the RB holds a impact shield. On command from the coach, the other DP, the tackler, assumes the proper defensive football stance. On command from the coach, the Tackler runs and form tackles the other player and drives player backwards for 5 yards.

RB

T

Defeat the Blocker and Tackle

The coach has the two bags on the ground in a straight line. One offensive player (OP) is at end of each bag. The first offensive player is the blocker (B). The blocker has a shield and the second offensive player is the runner (RB). The RB has a football. On command from the coach, the defensive player (T) runs down the bag and defeats the block. The defensive player continues down the second bag and tackles the RB and drive five yards.

Drill Coaching Point: Maintain proper position for the hit, keep feet apart along the bags and at point of impacts.

RB

B

T

Tackling to the Hole

Place the tackling dummies in parallel about three feet apart. A coach stands behind the tackler and points to the hole he wants the ball carrier to attack. At the coach's signal both players shuffle sideways until the ball carrier gets to the hole indicated, where he charges forward. The tackler should meet him in the hole and drive him backwards with a good form tackle.

Drill Coaching Point: Form tackle, good lift, drive hard.

RB

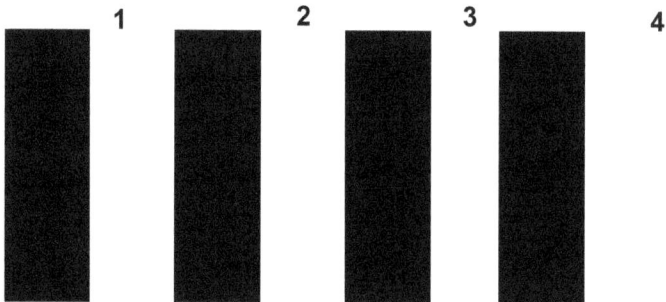

T

COACH

Tackling – Open Field

Set up two cones five yards apart. Set one cone is 2 yards from the first cone and set one cone 1 yard away from the second cone. Have RB behind first cone and LB behind second cone at 5 yards. On the whistle one, the coach has both players run to closest cone and breakdown with chop. The coach gives RB direction. On second whistle, RB goes L or R. On third whistle, the defender goes to make the tackle.

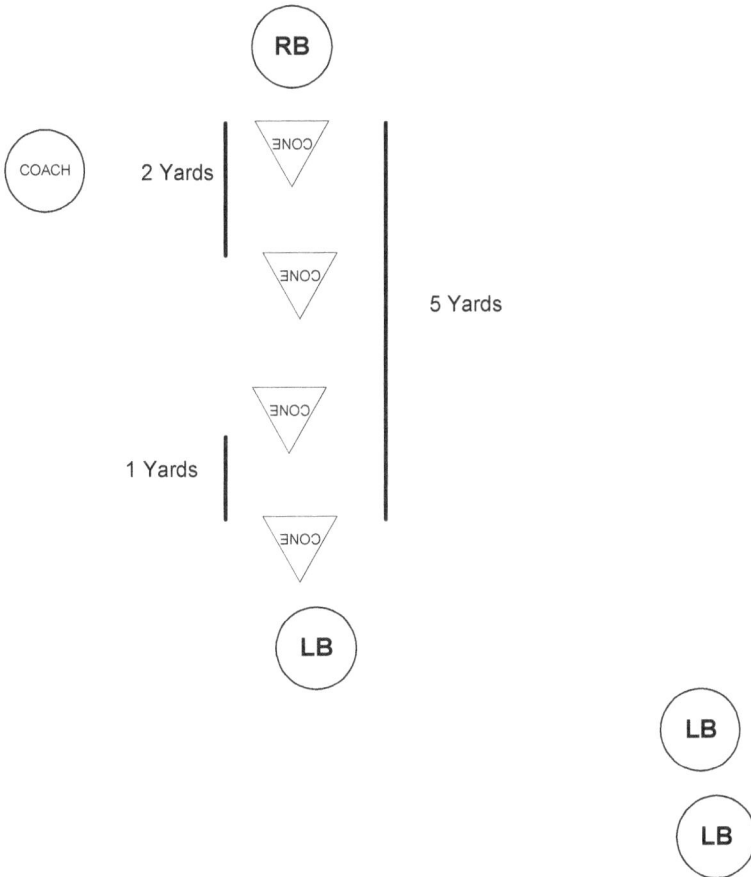

Tackling Open Field

Set one bag in middle of a yard line. Place runner (RB) on yard line and tackler (T) on other yard line 10 yards apart. On the command from the coach command, RB and T sprint to the bag. The RB makes a cut off the bag left or right. The T pursues the RB and makes the tackle

Drill Coaching Point: Tackler makes sure open field tackle.

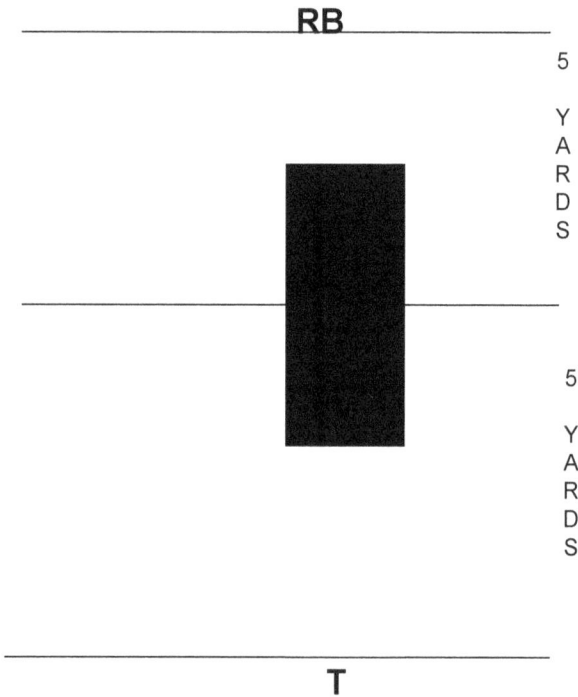

RB

5

Y
A
R
D
S

5

Y
A
R
D
S

T

Tackling Open Field

Set up a box 2 x 2 yards. Arrange the players around the outside so that each player is facing across from a player of roughly equal size. The coach will signal to a set of two players or coach can throw ball to RB. At his gesture, the object is for one player to make it across the box, while the other player must tackle him to prevent this.

Progression: Coach can make the box bigger to 5x5 yards.

Game: Have players keep score by giving one point to defensive player that prevents the runner from making it across the box.

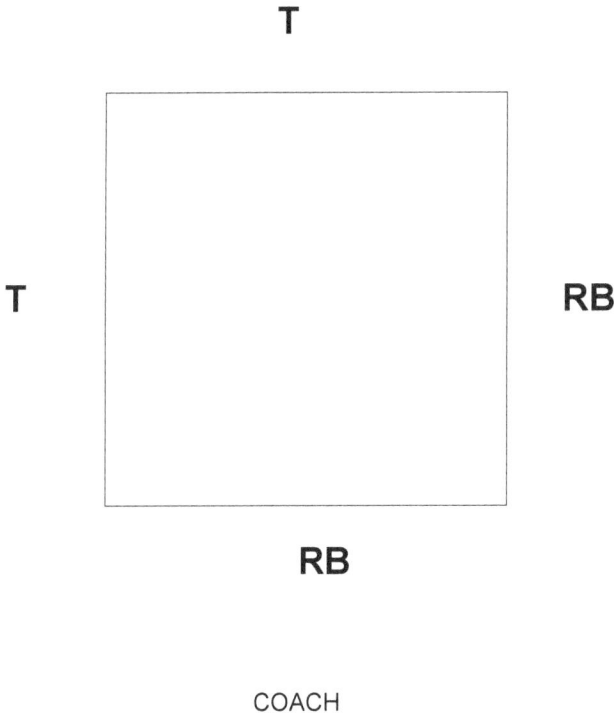

T

T   RB

RB

COACH

Tackling Sideline

Place runner (RB) on yard line and tackler (T) on other yard line 10 yards apart. Place cones 2 yards inside of sideline and one yard from middle yard line. On coach command, RB and T sprint to the cones. The RB makes move off the cone. The T should try to cut move to inside and force RB to sideline, pursue the RB and make the tackle or force out-of-bounds.

Drill Coaching Point: Tackler makes sure RB must go toward the sideline.

Game: Have players keep score by giving one point to defensive player that makes a good sideline tackle.

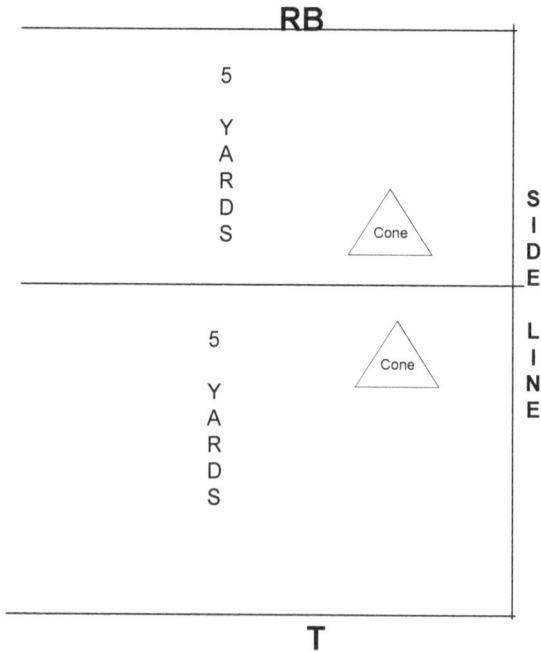

Tackling Gang

The two defensive players (DP) tackle the offensive player (OP). One goes low (first) and the other goes high (second).

Progression: Coach can use drill to practice stripping the ball.

OP

Coach   DP   DP

Tackling Goal Line

Place two cones three to five yards apart on any given line, representing the goal line. Place one defense player with his heels on the goal line. The ball carrier lines up 2-3 yards in front of him, holding a ball. On command the ball carrier starts and tries to break the plane between the cones, while the defensive player has to prevent touchdown.

Game: Coach can make it more competitive by keeping score. If the RB get over the line, the RB gets s point. If the tackler prevents a touchdown, the tackler gets a point. Play the game until one player reaches 5 points. Coach can move the RB to 5 yards.

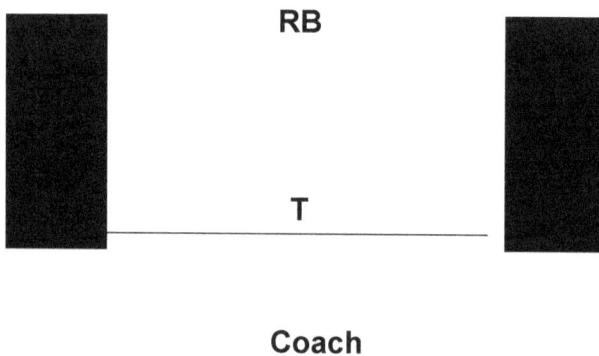

RB

T

Coach

Pursuit Linebackers Lane Drill

Place linebackers in position. Coach can use chutes or bags or cones to make sure linebacker are in position. Linebackers attack and react to flow to/away or counter read to lanes.

Drill Coaching Point: Coach makes sure linebackers stay in lanes, attack and react, and keep pads low.

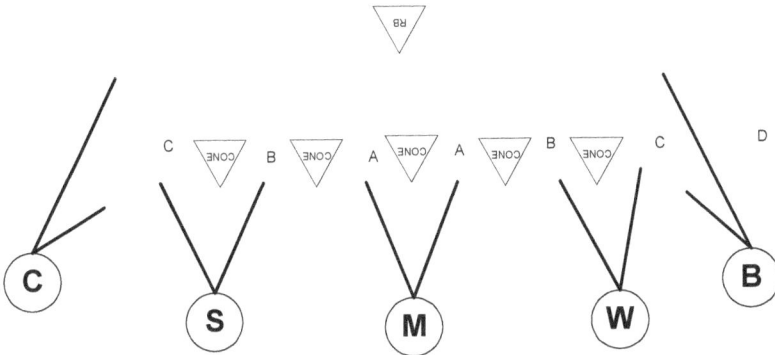

Strip Ball

RB holds the ball and the DP tries to strip the ball using punch or pull techniques. In the punch technique, the DP uses opposite arm to ball to get control of RB and DP punches the ball from the backside. In the pull technique, the DP uses opposite arm to ball to get control of RB and DP tries to rip the ball out of the RB's arm by pulling on the tip of the football closest to the RB's armpit.

Progression: RB runs toward DP. The DP makes the tackle the second DP come in and strips the ball.

Drill Coaching Point: Tackler must make sure of tackle first before attempting to strip the ball.

Fumble Recovery

The defensive player (DP) get in position. The coach drops the ball. The DP falls on the ball and secures the ball.

Progression (scoop and score). The DP tries to scoop and score. This drill can be added to many other drills.

Drill Coaching Point: Coach must ensure players understand when to fall on the ball and when to try to scoop and score. Generally, a coach wants a lineman to fall on the ball and linebackers to try to scoop and score. If the ball is fumbled around many players it is best to fall on the ball. A player that tries to scoop and score MUST be sure of securing the football.

COACH

DP

Stance and Backpedal

The coach has the defensive backs (DB) spread out in one line facing him. On command from the coach, the DBs assume the proper defensive stance. On command from the coach, the DBs backpedal maintaining a good position.

Stance Turn and Run

The coach has the DBs spread out in one or more lines facing him. On command from the coach., the DBs assume the proper defensive stance. On command from the coach, the DBs start backpedal while looking at the coach. The coach moves the ball back left or back right. The DBs turn hips in direction of coach's command and run. The DBs stay in straight line while turning and flipping.

Stance Direction

The coach has the DBs spread out in one or more lines facing him. On command from the coach., the DBs assume the proper defensive stance. On command from the coach, the DBs run in their stance in different directions maintaining a good hitting position.

Stance Angle Backpedal

The coach has the DBs spread out in one line facing him. On command from the coach., the DBs assume the proper defensive stance. On command the coach, the DBs backpedal for five yards maintaining a good position. On command, DBs angle backpedal 5 yards left. On command, DBs angle backpedal 5 yards left. On command turn and sprint final 5 yards.

Progression: DBs on command move feet quickly in place. Then the coach gives directions to move left, right, back and forward or vary to up and down. On go the DBs do a forward roll and sprint past the coach.

FS

DB   DB

Coach

Drill Coaching Point: Push off the back foot without false step. Maintain proper alignment and stance at all times (STAY LOW). Do not cross feet when changing direction.

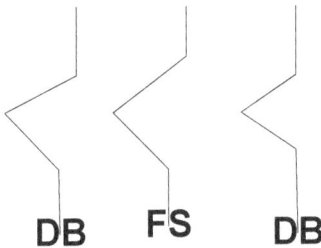

DB   FS   DB

Coach

Backpedal Tag

The coach has the defensive backs (DB) spread out in a line facing the coach. Also receivers (R) are placed in front of DBs at 5 yards. On command from the coach, the DBs start to backpedal and the receivers start running at the DBs. The receivers run until they tag the DB. The DB works at getting back as far as possible before the receiver's tag.

Progression: Place DB and R 2 yards apart with R at on a yard line. R tries to tag DB before the DB reaches next yard line.

DB   DB   DB

R   R   R

Coach

Pass Coverage - Zone Drops

Linebackers

Align linebackers (LB) in basic positions. Practice cover 3 drops. Call blitzes. Coach throws passes to different LBs.

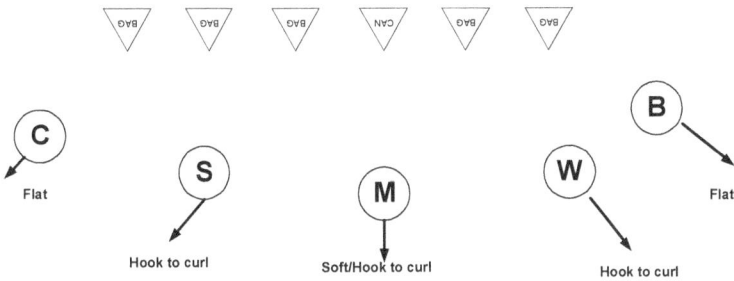

Defensive Backs

The coach has the DBs spread out in positions with two CBs and Free Safety. On command from the coach, the DBs start backpedal while watching QB/Coach. When the QB/Coach shows pass, The DBs turn and run to zone position.

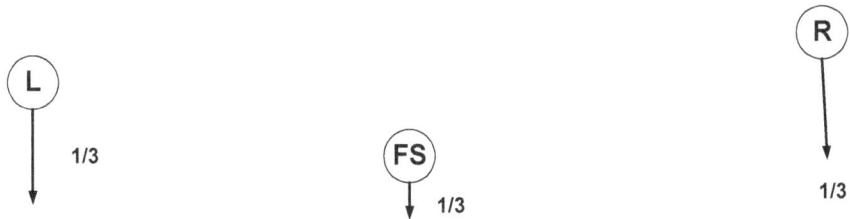

Pass Coverage Zone Cover 3

The coach has the DBs spread out in positions with two CBs and Free Safety. There is QB and two Receivers. On command from the coach, the receivers run deep routes. DBs start backpedal while watching QB/coach. When the QB/coach shows pass, the DBs turn and run to zone position. The QB throws a pass to one of the receivers, The DBs react.

Drill Coaching Point: Defensive backs never let receivers get behind coverage.

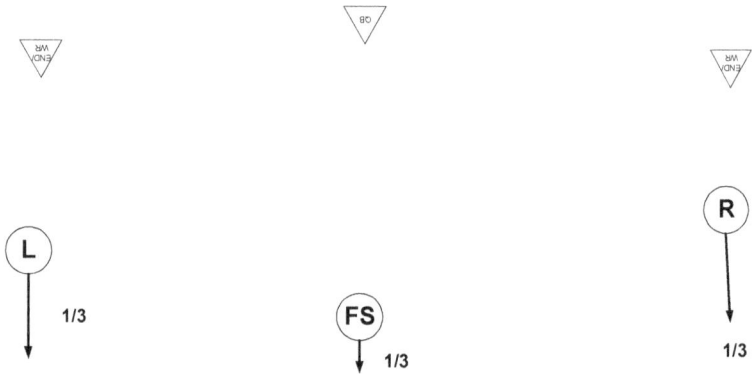

Team Defense Plays

Align defense in basic 3-5-3 alignment. Place bags for guards and tackle. For the center, place bag and use ball on a stick to center. Have one player be the tight end and switch sides randomly (strong/weak). Coach calls plays. Players run to gap. Players that are blitzing run to backfield. ADVANCE: Do one set all runs and do one set all pass. Coach can throw a passes to CBs to keep interest.

Drill Coaching Point: The drill is not only great for players' to perform defensive plays, but it is also good of conditioning. Coach makes sure the player perform assignments properly, but the coaches should promote a quick tempo.

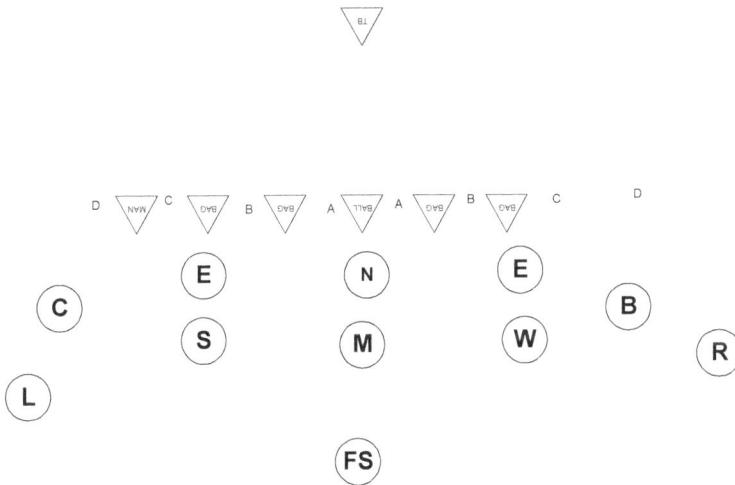

TE

D   MAN C   BAG   B   BAG   A   BALL   A   BAG   B   BAG   C   D

C   E   N   E   B
     S   M   W   R
L

FS

NOTE: This drill should be the last drill before team at every defensive practice. Coach should try to do all defensive plays two times. The first time assuming run and the second time assume pass.

Fun is the Word

At the youth level it is essential to keep it fun. Coaches must always remember, it is about the players. These players are 6 to 14 years of age. Everything must be geared to the specific age of the players. This is especially true of practice and drills.

CHAPTER 7
COACH GAME-DAYS

COACH GAME DAYS

Game days are the time to coach the team. At the youth and middle school levels, it is the time for players to learn game situations. It is time for players to perform his or her best. The following is an outline for coaching game-days.

Get players prepared

Analyze game plan

Make adjustments

Encourage positive outcomes

Game Coaching

Coaching involves the process of planning, preparing, performing and probing. This is a continuous process during the season. This same coaching process must be followed for game day. The coach must:

➢ Plan for the specific opponent

➢ Prepare the players and the team

➢ Perform during the game

➢ Probe during the game to make adjustments

Figure 14 shows the coaching process.

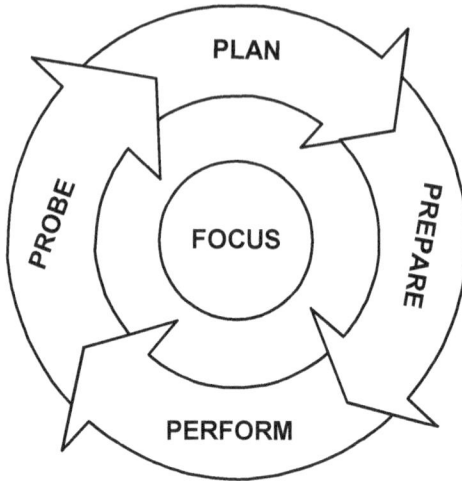

Figure 14. Coaching Process.

GET PLAYERS PREPARED

On game day, the coach needs to ensure the team is ready for the game. This requires preparing the players for the game both physically and mentally. During the pre-game, coaches should consistently focus on each individual player to ensure he/she is ready to play. At the youth level, young players can have many distractions. Therefore, focusing the players on the game can be a challenge. Keep in mind, many games are lost or won during the pre-game preparation.

Before the game, the coach ensures the team believes; establishes a game day structure; keeps the team focused on football, orchestrates the pre-game, reinforces the game plan with the coaches and players and energizes the team. The following summarizes the before the game actions:

Believe in victory

Establish a game day structure

Focus on football

Orchestrate the pre-game preparation

Reinforce the game plan

Energize the players and team

In order to ensure the team is prepared for the game day. It is a good idea to have game day preparation as part or whole of last practice before the game. The game day preparation practice should include:

- Pre-game structure
  o Game day warm-up
  o Position preparation
  o Team preparation
- Situations plays
- Substitutions
- Game tempo

Pre-game Preparation

The pre-game preparation should be a structured ritual. This is especially necessary at the youth level where players are accustomed to organization of activities. Also, this may reduce the anxiety of a game day for many players. Further, the team that looks good plays good is an old axiom that is true today. Your pre-game ritual could have an mind-set effect on the other team coaches or players.

Coaching Point: The coach should try to make the pre-game a set amount of time of around 30 – 45 minutes.

Physical Preparation

Physical preparation starts the pre-game ritual. It is critical during this time that the coaches provide the players the opportunity to get ready for the game.

Warm-up as Team

Coaches should have a warm-up routine for pre-game. At the youth level, a dynamic warm-up is usually sufficient. At the middle school level, a stretching routine might be added. The following is a sample dynamic warm-up routine:
- Form Run
- High Knees
- Butt Kicks
- Frankenstein Kicks
- Lunges
- Over-Under
- Power Slides
- Bounding (Frog Jump)
- Power Skip Shuffle
- Carioca
- Backpedal
- Toe Walks
- Heel Walks

Position Preparation

Defensive Line
- Stance
- Movement
- Step and rip (right and left)
- Form tackle
- Stunts

Linebackers
- Stance

- Movement
- Stun
- Form tackle
- Blitz
- Interception

Defensive Backs
- Stance
- Movement
- Form tackle
- Interception

Team Preparation
Defensive plays

Mental Preparation

Mental preparation is as important, maybe more important, at the youth and middle school levels. At most levels of football, a coach that knows the team can tell how the team will perform during the game by the team vibe during the pre-game. This is especially true at the youth level. In many games, the physical superior team does not win the game. The team that uses the head and heart has an advantage.

The pre-game speech should be different for every coach and every game. It should be appropriate to the coach's style and the team. The following are guidelines for a pre-game speech:

Share important information

Plan what you are going to say

Encourage the team

Avoid personal remarks

Keep team focused

ANALYZE GAME PLAN

Prior to the start of the game, the coaches should review the game plan. The coach must call the defensive plays during the game. The coach needs to put the player's in position to make plays on defense.

The defensive coach should plan specific plays to use against the week's opponent. For instance, the coach starts with 30 plays from the call sheet. For some opponent's the coach may know much about the opponent. The coach may highlight specific plays to use or may make a list of plays for the week. Another option is shown below, this game plan determines the play calls for a particular opponent for specific game situations. In addition, the plays for a specific game situation are listed in order of aggressiveness. For a first down and 10 yards situation, the most aggressive call is at the top of the list and the most conservative call is listed last. Some coaches may reverse the order. The important point is to have a plan.

Further, the coach needs to determine a quick call for each opponent. This is a call the defense uses for a situation when the defense cannot get a play call. This can be a no huddle by the offense or simply the defense did not get the call in time.

The following is a sample game plan call sheet for a specific opponent.

GAME PLAN FOR: _____

First Down (10 yards)

CALL	DL	Blitz	Cover
20	Slant **Strong**	Bang **To** - Lightning **To**	3
13/P	Stack **Strong**	Bang	3
14/P	Pinch **Strong**	Crack	3
16/P	Stack Weak	Ace To – Bang TO	3
23	Pinch **Strong**	Crack **To** - Lightning Away	3
28	Angle **Strong**	Lightning **To** - Blast **To**	1
1	Stack Weak	Ace **To**	3

Medium Yardage (more than 2 yards to 9 yards)

CALL	DL	Blitz	Cover
8/P	Angle **Strong**	Crack **To**	3
16/P	Stack Weak	Ace **To** - Bang **To**	3
21/P	Slant **Strong**	Bang **To** - Lightning **To**	3
14/P	Pinch **Strong**	Crack	3
27/P	Slant **Strong**	Lightning Away - Smoke Away	1
5	Stack **Strong**	Bang **To**	3

Short Yardage (less than 2 yards)

CALL	DL	Blitz	Cover
29/P	Stack Weak	Ace **To** - Bang - Lighting	3
24	Stack Weak	Ace **To** - Blast	3
13/P	Stack **Strong**	Bang	3
4	Slant Weak	Ace **To**	3

Long Yardage (Over 15 yards)

CALL	DL	Blitz	Cover
22/P	Angle **Strong**	Crack **To** - Lightning **To**	3
28/P	Angle **Strong**	Lightning **To** - Blast **To**	1
29/P	Stack Weak	Ace **To** - Bang - Lighting	3
1	Stack Weak	Ace **To**	3

Punt

CALL	DL	Blitz	Cover
13/P	Stack **Strong**	Bang	3

Extra Point

CALL	DL	Blitz	Cover
29/P	Stack Weak	Ace **To** - Bang - Lighting	3
25/ P	Angle Weak	Ace **To** - Crack **To** - Bang Away	3
24	Stack Weak	Ace To – Blast	1

Safe Any number from 1 to 9

Quick Call: 16

COMMENTS:

MAKE ADJUSTMENTS

Ideally, the team practices covered all the game situations and the coach will not have to make many game adjustments. The following is outline for coach during the game.

Display sportsmanship

Use all coaches and players

Remain focused

Implement the game plan

Nurture players' development

Guide the team and make adjustments

As a coach, you will need to make adjustments in every game. The objective at the youth level should be to limit the adjustment to the minimum necessary and make sure you plan for as many adjustments as possible. During the game, the coaches can make adjustment to players and the play. It is important to have a system to determine the following:

1. what adjustments are needed
2. who can make the adjustments.

As a minimum at the youth level, there must be player adjustments. First, some leagues may require a specific player playing criteria. Second, parental enthusiasm necessitates a game-day coach-player focus. Third, youth coaches should strive to maximize player participation.

Again, player adjustments require planning. The team that has 15 players does not have the same level of planning as a team with over 50 players. Yes, we had over 50 players on one youth team. Regardless, of 15 or 50 players, the coach needs to determine player's adjustment.

➢ Do you substitute one player for another player?

➢ Do you rotate players on every series or every play or certain situations?
➢ Do you substitute whole positions at a time? For instance, the team has a strong defensive line and a quick defensive line.
➢ Do you substitute teams at a time? For instance, one team is the silver team and the other team is the blue team.

Beside player adjustments, the coach usually will need to make some kind of play adjustment. Play adjustment must be limited to an adjustment that the players performed during a practice. Especially at the youth level, adjustments that are not practiced will result in failure by the player and mostly likely failure by the team. Coaches' should never set a player up for failure. They should as much as possible put players' in position for success.

During the first half, it is difficult to make major tactical adjustments. However, minor adjustments especially player adjustments are often necessary. Minor tactical adjustment can be made during the first half. However, most tactical adjustments are made at half time.

All tactical adjustment during the game should be made based on coaching observation. At the youth and middle school level, the coach usually does not have the luxury of other coaches in a observation spot with on-field head-sets for communication. Therefore, the youth coach must have some process to observe the other team to make adjustments. The following are some example of the process used to make observations to make adjustments. The first is a general game plan information sheet. Some of this information can be completed prior to the game. At the middle school level, the team may have to use the system of the high school. Therefore, the coach may know specific information about the opponent such as the type of offense. At the youth level, the opponent may or may not be tied to a certain system.

It is good to have a game planning system. The following form is a defense game plan to be completed by a coach once the game starts.

DEFENSE GAME PLAN

OPPONENT: _____

OFFENSE:

_____

QB: _____

Check center _____

DB: _____

SAFETY: _____

Run Game: _____

Passing Game: _____

POTENTIAL MISMATCHES:

_____

POTENTIAL WEAKNESS"

_____

GAME COMMENTS:

Beside the game plan sheet above, another tool to observe to the results of the defense to make adjustments is the defense call results sheet. The defense call results sheet evaluates the play of the defense play-by-play. The defensive coordinator in this defense must try to make the defense play call to counter the offense. The defense call results sheet allows the defensive coordinator to evaluate play calls in certain situations to make play adjustments.

DEFENSE CALL RESULTS SHEET

Situation		Call #	Result						
Down	Distance		Run			Pass			
			R	M	L	Comp	Incp	Gain	Loss

Defensive Adjustments

The following are some ideas for adjustments to game situation.

Adjustment for defensive line
> Stance
>> Three, two point or four point stance
>> Alignment of position
>>> Line up in gaps
>>> Move alignment
>>>> Line up defensive ends head up on guards
>>>> Move center head up on guard
>>>> Move defensive line over one position right or left

Adjustments of inside stack linebackers
> Alignment of position
>> Show – linebackers line up in blitz gap
>> Buzz – linebackers move in and out of gap
>> Stay – linebackers stay in basic position
> Middle linebacker spy a specific player

Adjustments of outside linebackers
> Alignment of position
>> Play on line of scrimmage
>> Play off line of scrimmage
> Coverage
>> Free safety take #2 on man-to-man defense

Adjustments for defensive backs
> Alignment of position
>> Play head-to-head
>> Play back to 7 yards

Adjustments for free safety
> Alignment of position
>> Play deeper 10 – 12 yards or prevent protection
> Use as spy for a specific player

ENCOURAGE POSITIVE OUTCOMES

Before, during and after the game, the coaches should be positive coaches. Positive coaches do the following:

Provide praise generously

Observe what players are doing right

Smile often

Interact with players

Treat each player fair and consistent

Identify each player by name

Validate individual self-esteem

Encourage sportsmanship

It is always easy to be positive after a win. It is critical to be positive win or lose.

Act the same win or lose

Focus on learning points (win or lose)

Talk up team

Ensure "team" integrity (do not single out any player(s)

Reinforce the positives

CHAPTER 8
KEEP IT SIMPLE

KEEP IT SIMPLE

The key to implementing the 3-5-3 defense at the youth and middle school level is to keep it simple. However, it is a mistake to underestimate the ability of youth players to get it right. Therefore, the coach should ensure the 3-5-3 defense is uncomplicated while at the same time stretching the players' capabilities.

The following are some guidelines to keep it simple.

Systemize the program

Instill a foundation

Motivate for the future

Plan everything

Learn to learn

Emphasize life skills

SYSTEMIZE THE PROGRAM

A system creates an organized environment. Every successful football team has a system. As a youth or middle school coach, a major objective must be to systemize your program. A system makes it easy to ensure coaches and players understand the program.

The following are guidelines to systemize your program:

Prepare the program

Recognize the importance of people to the program

Organize the program

Guide the program

Require a football system

Allow for changes to the program

Maintain the program

INSTILL A FOUNDATION

A solid foundation supports the football program. As stated in chapter one, the football program needs a solid foundation. A straightforward foundation supports the football team.
The following shows the element of a solid foundation.

Foster openness, fairness, and sincerity

Operate with honesty

Use common sense

Nurture trust

Demonstrate appropriate behavior

Allow involvement by everyone

Teach right from wrong

Instill values

Only do to others what you would want done to you

Never compromise ethics, integrity, or trust

MOTIVATE FOR THE FUTURE

Motivated players provide the future of football. In today's world, every football coach must be concerned with the future of football. Each coach's motivation must be to grow football for the future. Today's players have many options for the use of his or her time. Coaches must keep this in mind.

Motivation of players should be on the coach's mind always. There is anyways the conflict between classic coaching and modern coaching. Every coach must resist the temptation to use a negative (tear them down and build them up) style.

The following provides guidelines to motivate players.

Make it clear that the team has a shared goal

Orient the team toward the goal

Think about the team

Institute team recognition and rewards

Value individual player contributions

Avoid personal conflict with players

Take time to develop relationships with players

Encourage a sense of belonging on the team

PLAN EVERYTHING

Planning minimizes confusion. Planning also displays competence. Planning involves knowing your current situation, knowing what you want to achieve in the future, knowing the gap and working toward the goal.

The following gives an outline for action planning.

Provide understanding of where you are today

Learn where you want to go in the future

Analyze how to get from today to the future

Navigate to get to the future state

LEARN TO LEARN

Learning keeps a coach up-to-date. As a coach, you should be continuously learning new ideas. The most dangerous coach in youth sports is the coach that played some level of football in his or her younger years and he or she thinks they know everything about football.

Many youth coaches have not been involved in football since high school or college. For some this has been many years. Change is rapid in today's world. Football is not an exception. Many of the philosophies, processes, methodologies, techniques, drills, rules, play and so on are not appropriate for today's football or today's youth football player.

The following is a guideline for coaching development.

List learning objectives

Establish a system to learning

Allow development

Record learning activities

Name learning achievements

EMPHASIZE LIFE SKILLS

Football provides a special opportunity to teach and learn life skills. Although this is the last item in this book, it is likely one of the most important.

A coach has great influence on his or her players, especially young players. Life skills are learned best by example. As a coach, you must understand young players are observing you constantly. In addition, life skills development should be a planned effort throughout the football season.

The following shows some life skills that football can enhance.

Leadership

Involvement - teamwork

Focus

Empowerment

Self skills

Keep to itness

Improvement

Learn

Listen

Success

Appendix A
TERMINALOGY

Wide/Field- wide side of the field

Short/Boundary- small side of the field or the boundary side based on hash marks

Strong Run Side Call (Formation)- the strong call –based on tight end, strong run formation, or wide side of field on balanced offense formation.

Weak Run Side Call (Formation)- the side of the formation away from the "Strong" call

Strong Stunt - Nose Guard has "strong" side "A" gap

Weak Stunt - Nose Guard has "weak" side "A" gap

Stack - Defensive Ends move outside of tackle

Pinch- Defensive Ends pinch down towards their guards

Slant- Defensive lineman move towards the STRONG call

Angle- Defensive lineman move away from the STRONG call

Power- Defensive lineman line up in called gap

Ace- Mike linebacker "A" gap blitz

Bang- Right and Left linebacker "B" gap blitz

Crack- Right and Left linebacker "C" gap blitz

Lightning- Bear/Cub edge or "D" gap blitz

Smoke - Corner back gap blitz edge or "E" gap blitz

Blast - Free Safety blitz

Back- sets the Defensive backs deeper into the chosen coverage

Switch- tells the defense to change coverage or responsibilities in man coverage

Bingo - yell "BINGO" on an interception to tell the defense that we got interception to change to offense

Ric- right side is strong pass formation call. The side of the formation with the most potential receivers

Liz- left side is strong pass formation call. The left side of the formation is the most potential receivers

Show – Linebackers line up in gap to blitz.

Buzz – Linebackers move in and out to gap

Stay – Linebackers stay in basic alignment.

ABOUT THE AUTHORS

James H. Saylor, Sr. has vast experience coaching, training, and educating at the youth and middle school level. He has coached every level of youth football. Over the last 5 years, he has focused on using the 3-5-3 defense at the youth and middle school level. Jim is the founder of The Business Coach, a consulting firm focusing on helping organizations achieve their specific VICTORY. He has assisted many organizations in discovering, designing, developing and doing successful management systems. In addition, he has led, managed, coached, trained and facilitated many individuals and organizations in achieving their specific VICTORY. He has prepared and presented many highly proclaimed training seminars and workshops globally. Jim is a widely recognized leading champion of Total Quality Management in the 1980s and 1990s. Jim is the author of the *TQM Simplified,* and co-author of *Customer-Driven Project Management* published by McGraw-Hill. For further information about Jim's books, guides and workshops see website:
www.thebusinesscoach.org

James H. Saylor, Jr. has years of experience coaching youth, middle school and prep school football. He has coached with Coach Pop at the youth and middle school level of football.

Both Coach Pop and Coach Jim have coached youth and middle school football teams with success. Over the last five years, their teams have always had a winning record. In 2007, they won a youth league championship at the youth 100 pound level and they had an undefeated team at the middle school using the 3-5-3 defense

OTHER BOOKS BY JAMES SAYLOR

MANAGING FOR VICTORY

Are you looking to take your business, company, organization, department, agency or workgroup to a higher level of success? Now MANAGING FOR VICTORY a proven management system for achieving business results through superior customer satisfaction, organization excellence and progressive leadership. This management system can be implemented easily by small, medium and large companies. It works for private or public organization. Its verified processes, methods, tools and techniques work for service and manufacturing industries alike. This book provides the executive, owner, entrepreneur, manager, supervisor, lead and associate easy-to-understand processes to achieve specific VICTORY.

Being a Progressive Leader

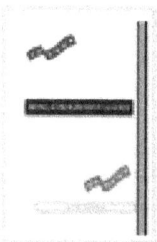

This is a introduction to *Being a Progressive Leader*. Specifically, progressive leaders':

Lead by example; **E**stablish a common purpose; **A**ct to develop a superior organization; **D**rive excellence; **E**nhance others, **R**einforce progress.

MANY MORE VICTORY GUIDES AT:

www.thebusinesscoach.org

.

www.ingramcontent.com/pod-product-compliance
Lightning Source LLC
Chambersburg PA
CBHW031257090426
42742CB00007B/491